Simple Business Strategies for *Sustainable* $uccess

Learn the 2% Shifts
and Hidden Skills for High-level
Achievement and Fulfillment

Alex Parker

Destiny by Design Business Strategist

Simple Business Strategies for Sustainable $uccess: Learn The 2% Shifts and Hidden Skills for High-level Achievement and Fulfillment© 2023 Alex Parker

All rights reserved. No part of this book may be reproduced, distributed, stored in a retrieval system or transmitted in any form by any means (including photocopy, recording, scanning, or other electronic or mechanical methods) except for brief quotations in critical views or articles and certain other noncommercial uses permitted by copyright law, without the prior written permission of the author, or the author's estate. For permission requests, write to the author at the address provided in the back of this book.

Print ISBN: 9798858863014

Publisher: **Author Writer's Academy**

AWA Literary Agency, United States

Senior Editor: Marjah Simon

www.AWA4Life.com

Cover Design and Illustrations - Author Writer's Academy

DISCLAIMER: The content in this book is intended for educational and entertainment purposes only. This book is not intended to be a substitute for the legal, medical, psychological, accounting, or financial advice of a professional. The author and publisher are not offering professional services advice. Additionally, this book is not intended to serve as the basis for any financial or business decisions. You should seek the services of a competent professional, especially if you need expert assistance for your specific situation.

Success stories and results shared are not typical and do not guarantee future results or performance. While best efforts have been made in preparing this book, the author and publisher make no warranty, representation, or guarantee with respect to the accuracy or completeness of the information contained herein. References are provided for informational purposes only and do not constitute endorsement of any websites or other sources.

The author and publisher assume no responsibility for your actions and specifically disclaim responsibility for any liability, loss, risk, or any physical, psychological, emotional, financial, or commercial damages, personal or otherwise, which is incurred consequently, directly or indirectly, of the use and application of any contents of this book.

The author reserves all rights to make changes and assumes no responsibility or liability on behalf of any purchaser, reader or user of these materials. Readers should be aware that the websites listed in this book may change or become obsolete.

The e-book version of this book is licensed for your personal enjoyment only. It may not be resold or given away to other people without a purchase of a copy for each recipient. Thank you for respecting the hard work of the author.

The ideas provided in this book are solely that of the author and do not necessarily reflect that of Author Writer's Academy.

For your **Complimentary Financial Statement Demonstration** 5-Part video series to accompany the mastery steps in this book, while available, visit
www.AlexParker.UK.com

Foreword

You know that feeling when you've reached the end of the long road trip or hike or maybe a recovery from a health setback, and while the journey was almost unbearable at times, you take great pride in what you've achieved?

With this book I take great pride in what Alex has achieved, not because I had anything to do with it but simply because I've watched his journey. I've seen what he's overcome. I've seen where he has reached. It's impressive.

Alex has been influential in my own journey from a young, somewhat inexperienced business owner, through to becoming the CEO of The Bissett Group of businesses, having established my reputation as an author, speaker, and global influencer along the way.

Having known Alex for nearly 20 years, I've personally benefited from his 40 years of experience and his qualifications as a Chartered Certified Accountant and Chartered Tax Advisor. He now also holds a Certificate in Professional Coaching Practice.

What sets Alex apart from most authors you'll read is that he is not a theorist. He is a practitioner. By this I mean that he walks his talk. He has suffered setbacks, just like you and me. He has come back stronger and most importantly, he's helped his clients to do exactly the same. I'm speaking from personal experience here.

In these pages therefore, you'll benefit from 'real life', 'in the trenches' style stories, advice and guidance - the type that I've benefited from personally for many, many years.

Alex's advice is something we can all learn from. He has taken the complexity out of success and streamlined the process for all of us. I can honestly say that I have never met a professional colleague (and I've met tens of thousands) who cares more or goes further to serve their clients. That has allowed a professional connection to evolve into a long-term personal friendship.

I wish you the very best of success as you take this journey with Alex. Having taken it myself, I can tell you that it leads to somewhere better than where you were at the start.

Martin Bissett, Manchester, England. Summer 2023.

Dedication

I stand on the shoulders of many of the great business and industry leaders who have come before me. I dedicate this book to you all.

To those who have impacted the world in ways that most can but dream.

To those who have shone a light for others in search of wanting more.

To those with the willingness to attain what many believe to be impossible.

To those who have guided me to the very heights I have reached today.

Thank you.

I put in an endless amount of hard work and long hours, and made a big investment of time and economics to learn from some amazingly successful people. And now, I get the opportunity to share what I have learned with you, my wonderful audience.

I would be remiss not to acknowledge my mentors' impact upon myself, and it is my true blessing to give them credit, as I now wish to do for others what they did for me.

I have also had the privilege to work with wonderful clients throughout my career as an accountant and business coach. While I have been working hard to help and serve them at the highest level, I have been honing my craft, so I am grateful to each and every client I have served along the way.

And finally, I would also like to dedicate this book to a brave little girl called **Kitty**, who our Heavenly Father called home to Him at the tender age of 9 years old. She was such a beautiful, brave, and inspirational soul who is deeply missed.

Kitty, you will forever live on in the hearts of all who knew you and you inspire us to create great things in your memory each and every day.

Acknowledgments

To my dad, **Ian Parker**, it was you who not only helped me with my math homework but prepared me for life. You are the foundation that set me on the course to achieve everything I have achieved mathematically, logically, and financially. I am so grateful to you for being the catalyst for my passion for serving, which fills my life today.

I am so thankful to the powerful teachers and thought leaders that have enabled me to bring this material to my audience:

Tony Robbins, when I discovered you, I was lost in the depths of despair. I attended my first UPW event in 2008, and you allowed everyone who signed up for Mastery University, including myself, to come on stage. I shook your hand and said, "Thank you for this opportunity." You replied, "This is just the beginning." I did not realize how prophetic those words would be, and ever since, I've wanted to meet you again to tell you how impactful those words were.

Your teachings shone a light that showed me a way into hope. Your big heart, powerful strategies, and willingness to serve are why I am who I am today. It is such a blessing that I get to pay it forward now. Thank you.

Keith Cunningham, you are a beautiful soul and such an inspiration. The very first time I heard you teach, you said, "I'm going to teach you two years' worth of Harvard accounting in two hours." As a CPA, I was intrigued and listened attentively. At the end of it, I realized you had fulfilled your promise. You took a complex topic and made it simple and easy to understand for the layperson. Your example is what I now get to do for my clients. Because of you, I get to share my love of numbers with business owners and change their lives. "Hello? God Bless Texas."

Jay Abraham, you are phenomenal. You know twenty words for every word I know! I love how you have helped so many people and cross-pollinate industries. It is my pleasure and privilege to bring some of your more basic strategies in this book to my audience. You are deeply inspirational and powerful in what you teach. I am forever grateful for the impact you help me to bring to my audience.

Without my powerful mentors, this book would not have been possible. Thank you for your inspiration, your teachings, and for being a great example of what's possible.

Letter From the Author

Dear reader,

First of all, I want to take a moment to thank you for investing your time into reading my book – an act I do not take lightly. In my experience, many people often talk about how they want to *improve* their lives, *build* their businesses, and *create* prosperity and fulfillment. Yet, how many really apply themselves to this goal versus those who give up somewhere along the way, settling for much less?

Let me be direct with you. Sadly, most people do not read the entirety of *any* book they pick up, let alone implement what they learn from it. Given this, I want my intention here to be clearly known. I do not wish to simply inform you nor to produce a book for mere entertainment purposes. Instead, my focus is directed toward influencing you to take direct action. I feel it is only right that I share with you that this is *not* a get-rich-quick scheme. It is unlikely that you will read this material once and go ahead and implement everything immediately, achieving instant results. But for the few who are:

- hungry for change
- prepared to keep coming back to this material
- willing to actively engage in the exercises I suggest
- able to clearly create a compelling vision
- committed to taking relentless action in the pursuit of their dreams

I believe I have valuable information to share with you, and it is my privilege to act as your guide on this journey.

I encourage you to take notes as you read this material rather than just reading passively. One of my coaches, Tony Robbins, has commented on research that has shown that if you just read or listen to new material passively, retention of such content is around 10% after 30 days. However, if you take notes as you learn something new, even if you never look at those same notes again, retention increases to 50–55% after 30 days. And if you are active as you learn something new, moving your body energetically (more on this later), it is possible to not only retain 80–90% a month later but also increase the likelihood of *implementing* what you learn – it is this very implementation that I truly desire for you, above all else.

For a moment, let's turn to some statistics. Sadly, most businesses don't make it. I have attended many Business Mastery events with Tony Robbins, who shared some very scary statistics for business survival – Tony told us 50% of all new businesses do not make it past their first year. After five years, only 20% remain in business, and after ten years, this drops to just 4%. This figure does not even necessarily indicate that the remaining businesses are successful and profitable but, instead, represents the number who survive.

Indeed, many people are not happy with their business performance or the current level of professional achievement in their lives. However, there are a few who truly excel in both, and my whole life's mission has been to study what makes these few so successful, modeling what they do in order to help others achieve the same results. My mission here is to help you *thrive* in business, not just *survive*.

I called my most recent business *Destiny By Design*™ because I want to help and guide my clients, my audience, to design their destiny purposefully. I love to help and serve people at the highest level, and that desire stems from my experience of having been personally defrauded, which I will discuss further in the book. I was wiped out and had to start again. It was such a painful experience, but that led me to all the business events where I learned some powerful strategies that have since shaped me into the man I am today. The speakers I have encountered shared from their hearts; they didn't hold back, and they gave me everything they had. And it was such that it saved me and helped me avoid bankruptcy; it allowed me to rebuild. Now, I want to pay this forward, that gift I received from these wonderful mentors I found. I'm very passionate about paying this forward to others; it is my driving force. I am committed to saving as many people as I can from going through what I went through.

The next year, five years, even ten years will surely pass and pass quickly – but the question I would ask you to ponder for a moment is this: Where will you be in that time? Will you carry on doing what you have always done or are you ready and willing to consider a new approach?

I'm sure you've heard that the definition of madness is continuing to do the same thing over and over, expecting a different result. Well, my invitation, perhaps even my challenge, to you, if you're ready, is to take time to ***design your destiny with purpose***, with forethought, with careful planning. And you do not have to do this alone because I am here to help and guide you every step of the way.

Ready to get started?

Okay, let's begin our journey together ...

Alex

Contents

Introduction	**1**
Why I Am Able to Help You	4
The Aim of This Book	13
PART 1: PSYCHOLOGY AND MINDSET	**19**
SECTION ONE: The Momentum Model	20
SECTION TWO: The Triad – The 3 Molders of Meaning	37
SECTION THREE: Three Foundational Principles of Business	55
PART 2: HOW TO UNDERSTAND AND READ FINANCIAL STATEMENTS	**71**
SECTION ONE: Seeing Beyond The Balance Sheet	72
SECTION TWO: Make a Statement Through Your Income Statements	85
SECTION THREE: Understand Your Cash Flow Statements, Realize Your Cash Potential	91
PART 3: BUSINESS STRATEGIES TO MOVE FORWARD	**105**
SECTION ONE: Leverage in a Business - The Difference Between Income and Yield	106
Leverage in a Business - Sales Strategy	114
Leverage in a Business - Cost Strategy	118
SECTION TWO: 10-10-10 Strategy	123
SECTION THREE: Build A Cash Machine	133
CONCLUSION	**139**
NEXT STEPS	**141**
ABOUT THE AUTHOR	**147**

Introduction

> *There is power in simplicity.*
>
> –Alex Parker

Let me ask you: Would you rather have a greater impact with your clients/customers or a greater income?

Here's another question: Why choose one when you can have *both*?

Just think for a moment. If I can show you how to make a small 2% change in an area of your business each week, this will produce a change of almost 300 % over the year. This is easier than you might think. With the simple strategies throughout this book, you will be empowered with everything you need to make that change a reality. So what are you waiting for?

I am delighted to have this opportunity to share with you my most effective business strategies, cultivated across a nearly-four-decade accounting and *Destiny by Design*™ business strategist career. Now, you need to do nothing more than let these principles guide you toward your financial *freedom* and *fulfillment*.

Having cut my teeth within and risen to the very top of the accounting profession, building my own firm from a mere concept to an industry leader, I now aim to share my wisdom with those I have spent my entire life trying to help and serve. For the past forty years, through my practice, I have enabled family-owned, small businesses to achieve and sustain financial success, teaching business acumen that enables both profitability and durability. Yet, as I contemplate how to best use my abilities to facilitate greater change, I realize the importance of distributing this knowledge to those outside my present client list. Through *Simple Business Strategies for Sustainable $uccess*, it is a privilege to share my expertise with an altogether wider audience.

This is my first book, and my intention is to present to you simple, powerful, and profound strategies that anyone hungry for more in their business and their life can apply straight after reading. After almost forty years of experience, I have developed a wealth of powerful strategies I can now share; however, I am very aware that too much information, especially within such an intricate and important subject as this, can often overwhelm. So as a great believer in the power of three, I have carefully considered the three most powerful elements that will allow you to build a foundation of business knowledge that can be built upon later:

- Psychology and Mindset
- Understanding Financial Statements
- Success Strategies

The next ten years will pass by, regardless of how you engage with them. So the question remains, are you going to rock up haphazardly at the end of these years or are you going to deliberately *design* your *destiny*?

That is what I am here to do: help you to design your destiny. So many people go through life on autopilot, and admittedly, I must hold my hands up, for I, too, was like that for so long. But each and every one of us must realize that we can actually take time away from the madness around us and create a compelling vision that will pull us forward. By allowing you to realize your own compelling vision, this book will show the ways to design your own destiny with purpose, clarity and power.

Why I Am Able to Help You

I am an Accountant/CPA and a Business Strategy Coach, and an expert in my field, so the terms in this book are familiar and easy to me. However, I'm aware that this may not be the case for many business owners. As such, I have made it simple, clear, and accessible. I have explained what these terms mean so that I can convey meaning when I'm discussing these topics. I want you to readily understand and not be confused with any terminology as you work through this book.

I have frequently seen that the ability to build sustainable success as a small business is one that few have been able to harness. An abundance of "how-to" business guides riddle the book market, declaring that they have the solution for long-term profitability and success. Yet each and every one of them ignores a fundamental aspect: the power that is within *you*.

I am privileged to have had the opportunity to learn both life and business skills from some of the most influential individuals on the planet. Combining my own knowledge, built through decades of experience, and theirs, I intend to share critical wisdom with those who have not had the fortune I have.

For all my life, I have worked 24/7, all year round, selling my time for money. This has brought me great individual success, creating the kind of financial comfort that would leave most content to see out such a career in relative peace. Yet I now realize that I have the opportunity to make a far greater impact by sharing the lessons I have learned from mastering the multi-faceted applications of business to an audience that truly requires and desires them.

Despite my success, something has always appeared to be missing. Sure, I have risen to the top of an industry many struggle to even enter, but I have always had a certain feeling of wanting more. I now realize that this "more" is the ability to serve—to serve small businesses, to serve those without hope, to serve *you*.

Both growth and contribution have been my main drivers throughout my life. I have now achieved all that I can in the industry I have dedicated my life to, leaving little room for further *growth*. It is now my chance to *contribute* everything I have learned to an entirely new audience and to enable *you* to have the kind of success that has allowed me to have this platform.

This has ultimately led me to find a new value proposition and a new way of serving others. I believe I can reach so many more through this very book, to later accompany state-of-the-art digital products that people will be able to access even when I am not there to deliver one-to-one support. This will also allow such expertise to reach an audience that will perhaps not have direct access to me but with whom I can still share my experience, knowledge, and material in magnitudes that, until now, I never thought possible.

Throughout my career, I have always had a passion to help and serve my clients at the highest level. This is founded on the fact that almost 15 years ago, I was defrauded. I made an error of judgment and trusted the wrong people. This occurred during a business acquisition, and I was almost left with nothing. I had bills to pay, payroll and loan obligations to meet, and little income coming in – it was a very dark and painful experience. I had to start again from scratch and thought it was the worst experience I could ever face. Yet now, I actually realize that it was a blessing because it gave me the opportunity to develop tools, strategies, and empathy that I would not have had otherwise.

I really know what it is like to be in that painful position where it seems as though your business is not going to work. Yet I found a way and now have the means to show you how to as well. My challenging experience emphasized the importance of having effective support to overcome such obstacles. So now, my heart calls me to step up in support of those who are either going through the same challenges in business that I did or have reached a plateau and want to move to the next stage.

During my time in the accounting industry, I began to notice a pitfall that many of my peers, and indeed myself for a while, repeatedly fell into. Many of us would frequently compromise between having a greater impact on our clients *or* increased income in our practice without realizing that both can be achieved simultaneously. I believe accountants are in a deeply privileged position; we are entrusted by our clients to oversee their finances, which I am sure you do not need me to tell you are such an integral part of business. Therefore, we are given a ready-made platform to deliver more than just financial statements.

Yet throughout my career, I came to learn that most accountants often know the price of *everything* but the value of *nothing*. This is to say that many disregard the financial and economic benefits of serving clients in more ways than any one basic value proposition. What was perhaps an even greater revelation was my increasing awareness that such notions could be applied to the approaches my very own clients were demonstrating in their own businesses. Ultimately, my end goal is to enroll each and every one of *you* to step up and serve your clients strongly with passion and conviction, which will, in turn, reap unimaginable financial rewards.

It does not matter where your own motivation comes from; now is the chance to attend to both your clients and your business in a more powerful and meaningful way.

As an accountant, I was taught from an early stage in my career that the value of my end product was based on the production of financial statements. Only when I became an entrepreneur did I realize this was merely the *first* step, not the *last*. I simply needed to shift my mindset to realize the potential of entirely new approaches for accelerating growth, beyond any one value proposition, both for the benefit of my *clients* and my *business*. I realized the importance of adding heart and soul to my services and now urge you to do so as well. Now is the time for you to shift your own mindset beyond profit and loss statements and find new approaches to expand and sustain revenue and growth.

I have had the fortune of being mentored by some of the most prominent and impactful business leaders in the world, these include Tony Robbins, Keith Cunningham, and Jay Abraham, to name just three. Through meaningful interaction, the role of a mentor is to demonstrate how results are achieved and provide the blueprint to enact these actions yourself. Any human interaction between one person and another allows those taking part to see the blindspots of their counterparts they themselves otherwise wouldn't see because, ultimately, we will *not see* what we *cannot see*.

Keith Cunningham is one of many truly successful business leaders I have been privileged to learn from, and he has a great expression I want to share with you now. He says, "Great business *operators* get tired; great business *owners* get rich!" Many small business owners are self-employed business operators rather than true business owners, as indeed I have also been for many years. I think the challenge for all of us is moving from a business operator to becoming a business owner.

I had previously thought this was a choice between one or the other, but I now realize that this is a continuum, a sliding scale, if you will. If you asked me to give up helping and serving my clients, this would be a massive ask; however, I am making a transition in my own business. I am recruiting extra resources to help my business to deliver the more routine accountancy services so that I can focus my time on stepping up strongly to share my knowledge, experience, and expertise to a wider audience. This book is just the first step in this process.

I have always believed strongly in developing personal integrity, walking my talk, and I would feel very uncomfortable attempting to teach powerful business strategies if I was not employing these same strategies in my business and my life. I'm not saying for a moment that I've got everything figured out, far from it; I'm a work-in-progress, the same as anyone. However, I do feel blessed to have learned from some great teachers, many highly successful business entrepreneurs and trainers, but also from my own clients, in helping and serving business owners for almost four decades. This hands-on experience has been invaluable in developing my understanding of new concepts, principles, and strategies, which I now get to share with you. I'm on the same journey as you, as I perfect and hone my skills to grow and scale my business while I get to help others do the same.

My aim for *Simple Business Strategies for Sustainable $uccess* is to provide you with this very interaction. To provide guidance that will allow you to identify what you are currently missing while pulling the veil from your eyes to see once again the potential for a successful business. A mentor should enable you to realize what is possible, clearing your vision to see the possibility for a brighter day. I urge you to allow me to be yours as we embark on a journey of business growth and sustainability.

While the information and tools imparted throughout this book can be utilized by every business person intent on building sustainability and profits, there will be a direct focus throughout on small businesses – those who are going through challenges, feeling lost, and aspiring for more. This is to support those working extremely hard but who are perhaps not currently employing the best strategies and require my external voice to come in and say, "There is a better way. Come and listen."

As I mentioned, a large part of my passion for businesses of this type derives from my direct engagement with them through my practice. However, while small businesses have always made up a large portion of my clientele, allowing me insights into the trials and pitfalls many experience, my own practice started once as a small business. In the beginning, I was simply a man and an office, without a clue on how to build sustainable growth. Yet I did, and you can too.

Typically, I have found that most small businesses, the very audience I wish to serve, do not have access to the type of guidance that has enabled my success from other, more expensive, or complex sources. Now, I stress that this is in no way an indictment or presumption of your current level of achievement. I have simply reached the stage where I can no longer watch those around me struggle while knowing I have the means to share a better way.

I am standing on the shoulders of many powerful and successful business strategists who have walked this path before and have guided me to where I am today. Furthermore, I will always endeavor to give credit to those from whom I have learned different strategies when these are shared with you. For now, I see it as my responsibility and opportunity to pass on both my wisdom and theirs to those most in need of realizing their true potential.

Indeed, my empathy for such businesses also derives from having walked an entrepreneurial path, not having the time nor financial means to attend business courses or better educate myself on effective contemporary strategies, all the while knowing these would grant me great benefit. Yet I am now able to bring such resources to others in a medium I never had access to.

It is business owners and operators who frequently work the hardest yet do not employ the best strategy. Perhaps now is the time to allow an external guide to come in and show you that there is a better way.

My dad used to say, "If something's worth doing, you do it well." I have since learned another expression: *if something's worth doing, it's worth doing poorly.* Don't be afraid to make mistakes while you're looking to build a better tomorrow. Ultimately, it is better to get started, innovate, iterate, and refine instead of simply holding back and hesitating because you are afraid to fail. By reading this book, you will give yourself the opportunity to never have to look back again and to develop a future that will facilitate sustainable growth.

By implementing what I share with you here, you will be able to bring your mindset and, in turn, your business into a position where it can generate and accelerate, not just successful growth, but *sustainable* growth. In time, and with consistent adherence to the strategies and guidelines I will lay out for you, you will be able to go even deeper than you thought possible, all the while generating more funds and serving more clients, to reach the pinnacle of your industry without working 24/7.

The Aim of This Book

I have designed this book so that each chapter builds upon the last step-by-step, so I highly encourage you to read this book in the order it is written to get the most from it. Please do not skip around to what you think is easiest or to just the section you think you need. I have been very methodical and thoughtful in the way that I have put this book together so that you, the reader, will get the greatest benefit from it. If you try to implement the strategies but skip the mindset and understanding the numbers, you will not be able to implement the strategies successfully. I've seen it time and time again; you will not get the results. It would be such a shame to have established the strategies without all of the tools and equipment with which to maximize on that effort and investment of time and energy.

While these initial concepts may seem a little tiresome to learn in comparison to the more sexy business strategies imparted in the conclusive section of the book, I urge you to acknowledge their importance. These are the building blocks that will increase the likelihood of being able to implement and sustain the strategies provided later on.

As a strong believer in the rule of three, I naturally decided to organize this book as such. Split into three parts, each including three chapters, this book will provide a holistic and unified approach to business that taps into the psychological, administrative, and strategic aspects that each of its "competitors" does not.

The book's first section will outline the importance of psychology and mindset in business. Before being able to apply business strategy to our own businesses, we must first garner the necessary psychological mindset that will allow such strategies to be sustainably implemented. So often, the solution lies outside the comfort zone, on the other side of our fear. We have to move through our fear to be able to realize that solution. In this introductory section, I will share with you how to deal with these fears.

The first chapter will introduce you to the *Four Wheels of Motivation*, demonstrating what you are currently missing in your own approach to business. Chapter Two will follow with a revolutionary Triad approach to business motivation, demonstrating the importance of three notions: *Language and Meaning, Focus, and Physiology.*

After you learn these three steps, inspiration need not be a concern any longer as you explore your own business potential. This will lead into Part One's conclusive chapter, turning to the *Three Foundational Principles of Business*, which will encompass: knowing your ideal client, creating irresistible offers, and then over-delivering to create raving fans and a brand.

After demonstrating the importance of psychology and mindset in business, the book's second section will reveal the importance of understanding your own financial statements. The predominant client base for my accounting practice has been small businesses – the very people I hope to reach with this book – and throughout my engagements with such businesses, a range of common challenges have become apparent to me.

Crucially, many of these businesses appear to have a lack of understanding of their financial statements. Traditionally, I will present the financial statements, to which they will say, "How much have I made? What's my tax bill? Where do I sign?" That's usually where most people's strategy starts and ends: getting it done, signing it, and closing their eyes in the hope that one day their profits will equal their cash.

It soon became clear that most of my clients had little understanding of their financial statements and instead were content to focus on just one figure – the bottom line – which you will discover as you read on is just a theory, not a fact! Yet understanding your own financial statements is such an integral part of understanding your *own* business and industry in order to build and sustain success.

In this second section, I wish to enable you to not only learn how to read your financial statements but to then understand both where and how to employ little tweaks, small 2-millimeter shifts, that will improve your business in powerful ways. These are simple tools that will enable positive financial change. This will include things such as teaching the difference between income and yield, looking at leverage in a business, and understanding cash flow management.

It is important to realize that before successful business strategies can be implemented, you must first grasp these fundamentals of business psychology and documentation before attacking what you actually need to apply. These first two sections will set you up perfectly to do so before moving into the book's conclusive section: *Business Strategies To Move Forward.*

This will be a culmination of all the building blocks provided to you up to that point and how these can be brought together within direct, immediately applicable strategies that will accelerate your business growth in a sustainable way. This will include chapters on the importance of profit margins, the power of leverage in a business, and the 10-10-10 business strategy that I first learned from Tony Robbins, who I believe got it from Jay Abraham, and culminating in my final strategy, how to build a cash machine.

The reason I have chosen the picture of a plane for my website and this book cover is that I often liken running a business to that of a plane pilot. Did you know that most of the time, a plane is off course? It is only the constant corrective actions of the pilot/navigation system that allows the plane to arrive at its destination.

Just like a pilot, we have an array of dials and instruments to show us results (our financial statements), and we have a variety of levers that we can pull (our business strategies) to plot our course and arrive at our destination. This is why I first invest a little time with you on how to understand and read your financial statements before then sharing my business strategies with you.

Each section, combined, will culminate in a strategic resource you never knew you needed, until now. And after engaging and interacting with the content I will provide to you throughout, you may find yourself frustrated that it has taken you this long to find a guiding solution of this kind. Please take heart, you are here now, and my focus is all about delivering the maximum value to you, my reader, to enable the implementation of strategies shared within to help you achieve high-level, sustainable success and fulfillment in both your business and your life.

My careers, coaching, and faith have led me to this point in time; to use the old adage: *right place, right time*. Though it may seem a little cliché, I truly feel this is where I am. It is a calling, one from every little experience that has brought me to where I am today, to step up in a new and powerful way. I wish not to waste anything that has come before but instead to learn from it *all* and deliver this expertise to a new audience in a revolutionary way.

Guiding you to financial freedom and fulfillment, please allow me to take you on an adventure to discover the possibilities of business you never knew possible.

Yes, you're ready! So, let's get started …

PART 1
PSYCHOLOGY AND MINDSET

Without a strong mindset and psychology,
it doesn't matter how wonderful
a strategy I share with you, dear reader.
You will not implement it.
My purpose here is to get you
to implement the strategies because
I'm all about the end result.
It's not about the process;
it's all about how I can deliver an outcome,
a powerful result to you.
It is the foundation of a strong mindset
and strong psychology that will give you
the most opportunity to implement
the strategies and achieve the outcome you desire.

PART 1

SECTION ONE

The Momentum Model

> *The bottleneck of any business is 80% psychology and skill set of the business owner, and 20% strategies.*
> *– Tony Robbins*

I have always been passionate about my self-development. From the earliest stages of my career, I acquired as many audio programs as I could to learn new strategies and techniques to improve both my life and my business. Building upon this, I later progressed to attend masterclasses with some of the world's best industry leaders, taking my understanding of business strategy to a whole new level. Immediately, one common theme became apparent across all of this material as each and every one first stressed the importance of psychology and mindset. Only once this was established would these coaches proceed to share direct and specific strategies.

Now, I believe it is often just as powerful, if not at times even more so, to share both our mistakes as well as our successes. So, here is the first mistake I made when establishing myself as a *Destiny by Design*™ business strategy coach. Initially, I thought, "I can't teach psychology and mindset to my clients!" Such a topic sounded so fluffy and even a little irrelevant, especially to a so-called "serious" accountant and business coach!

But what I soon began to notice was no matter how powerful the business strategies I shared were, they would only be successfully implemented by my clients when they first had in place a strong psychology and mindset. So, I had to overcome my embarrassment over sharing what at first appeared to be the furthest thing from a powerful business strategy component. Indeed, I had to improve my *own* psychology and mindset before even considering teaching this subject to others!

My entire focus is to help you deliver *results* demonstrable through clear, measurable improvements. Therefore, the best place to start is by sharing what I have learned about psychology and mindset to ensure that when I later share my strategies with you, these will be implemented. As Tony Robbins likes to say: *"implementation trumps knowledge every day of the week!"*

This is a vast subject, but I have given much thought to the three most powerful and effective psychological and mindset tools I can share with you. And the first starts with the titular concern of this chapter: *the Momentum Model*.

I believe we all need a higher purpose in life; a hunger and a drive for more. A calling, if you will, to keep going even when times are tough. Yet, we also need tools we can use to achieve this, and I have found that one of the most effective is this very model. The secrets within it underpin, to a large extent, just why the rich get richer and the poor get poorer, and I am not *just* talking about financial riches. I believe this also applies to all areas of our life.

I learned this from Tony Robbins, who first introduced me to the Momentum Model. I would like you to draw out four circles on a piece of paper, two at the top and then two more underneath. In the circle at the top left of your page, please write the word: POTENTIAL. In the circle at the top right of your page, write the word: ACTION. In the circle at the bottom left of your page, write: BELIEF/CERTAINTY. And in the final circle at the bottom right of your page, write the word: RESULTS. Then draw arrows in a clockwise direction connecting all four circles in a bigger circle. This is shown in the image below, but I urge you to draw it for yourself.

I want to do everything I can to encourage you to derive the most benefit from everything I share with you. So, throughout this book, I will encourage you to draw out all my diagrams yourself on a notepad since this will aid your understanding and retention.

MOMENTUM MODEL

```
        POTENTIAL  →  ACTION
            ↑              ↓
        BELIEF/    ←   RESULTS
        CERTAINTY
```

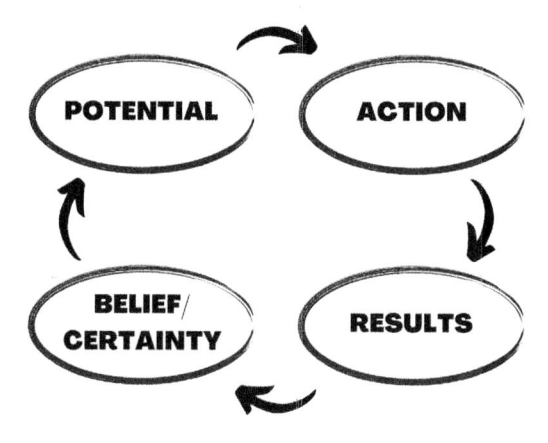

You will see that there are four components of the Momentum Model:
- Beliefs/Certainty
- Potential
- Action
- Results

Beliefs/Certainty

What is belief? It's a thought or a feeling we habitually think we have absolute certainty about. We don't actually experience life. We instead experience what we believe is happening in that moment. So, we have the power inside of us to change our beliefs at any moment. We master our outer world by mastering our inner world (beliefs) first.

Potential

We all have the capacity to perform in various areas to a depth that we may not yet realize. I believe our potential is unlimited. If you look at someone that has achieved what you want to do, it shows us that it is possible for us too. I also believe that we have a deep well of untapped, latent potential, and I am here to help you to fill your bucket and overflow.

Action

True action is not just dabbling. It's making a consistent, committed movement toward your objective. It is taking decisive, massive action, not just playing on the edges. We are relentless until we reach our destination. Action is not just trying a couple of things and giving up when it doesn't immediately work. It's seeing it through to completion.

Results

I am passionate about results. People are not interested in our process or service. They are interested in the outcome of our committed actions. Everything we do is because we want to create a certain experience, outcome, or achievement. We are creators that have the beautiful ability to create something that wasn't there before. So, what have you achieved, manifested, and produced from your movement?

Which do you think is the most important element in this model?

People often answer that they think action is the most important element. It is true that the amount of action we take has a direct impact on the results we achieve. However, this is only the case when the specific actions we choose move us directly closer to the results we desire. I believe we all have massive potential to tap into direct and effective action, yet most often seem unable to do so. Yet why is this?

I put forth to you the notion that if we lack belief or certainty or if we have doubt and are fearful, we will not be able to tap into much of our potential. In turn, this will lead us to where we are unlikely to take much action, culminating in results we do not desire. Often when I coach clients, they tell me they can't do something, that they have tried *everything*, and it still doesn't work. Yet when I enquire as to what it is that they tried, they often describe to me only one or two things before being discouraged and giving up.

> ***Whether you think you can***
> ***or you think you can't***
> ***– you're right.***
> **– Henry Ford**

If you believe you can't do something, it's game over. I am sure you know this, so now we merely have to find a way to increase our belief and sense of certainty. This will allow us to tap into more of our potential and take more action to achieve better results.

So, how do we increase our sense of certainty? One way to achieve this is by practicing ... we all get rewarded in public for what we practice in private. Another way is to take more action, something I am a great supporter of. However, if we feel uncertain, then such action won't be as powerful or effective as it could be. Instead, the secret to creating a shift and increasing our positive momentum, and thereby our results, is to envisage results in our minds ahead of time.

Our mind cannot distinguish between something we vividly imagine with feelings and emotion and something we actually experience if we do it enough times. This is a notion that has been known in the area of sports for many years. I like to follow Formula 1 motor racing, and I often see drivers sitting in the cockpit with their eyes closed before they set off on their laps. And what are they doing? They are imagining driving the perfect lap – and we can employ this technique in our daily lives too.

It does not matter how many actions we take if our *beliefs* aren't powerful and positive. Indicative of suboptimal psychology and mindset, it will not matter how wonderful the strategy is because our *potential, actions,* and *results* will ultimately not be realized. Belief is the very foundation of our psychology and mindset and will be a constant theme integrated throughout my teachings.

In my experience, many clients simply think that beliefs are absolutes. That what they believe is set in stone, something they are stuck with and are impossible to remedy. But now is the time to control change by realizing that we, in turn, can control what we believe.

In life, whether aware of this or not, we constantly make decisions as to what to believe. I believe we are continually asking ourselves three important questions about everything in every moment of our life:

- What do I believe?
- What does this mean?
- What am I going to do?

In this chapter, along with an understanding of the Momentum Model, I will share with you each of these concepts that I believe are foundational to your beliefs in order to enact and realize your *own* greatest potential, actions, and results.

Now, deciding what is possible is entirely dependent upon what we believe something means. For instance, if I say, "Oh, I can't do that," that's it. Game over. Whereas if I were to say, "I can do anything, and there must be a way," this would be a far more empowered state to be in. It allows me to face whatever challenge it is with strength, power, and conviction.

Each of us has that choice at every moment. Yet so often, we are not aware that we have that choice until somebody arrives to tell us about it. Well, I am here now to tell you that you will always have a choice to believe whatever it is you set your mind toward.

I believe we all have the potential to do far more than we realize. And if we see somebody else excelling in an area that we ourselves wish to, that shows what can be possible for us. That there is *potential* there for us to do that, as well.

Consider for a moment the 4-minute mile. Before Roger Bannister accomplished this feat in 1954, no athlete had accomplished this feat. After he achieved this, multiple athletes have since achieved this. Why is this? I believe that Roger Bannister showed everyone else that it was possible, which increased the belief in other athletes that they could also achieve this.

But in order to replicate these results, we need to understand what it is they are doing and model these actions. Potential can always be found simply by observing the world around us, but in order to access it, we need to start with our mindset, with our belief, and to believe that it's possible.

Indeed, the Momentum Model very much starts with our belief. Because if we don't have this belief – the strong trust in ourselves that we can do something – we will be unable, in turn, to harness our full potential. This then leads into our actions, whereby doubting our own potential will lead to a lower, sub-optimal implementation of our actions. This will then lead to disappointing results, causing our belief and certainty to reduce, thus perpetuating a cycle of self-doubt and mediocrity.

But, if we can work on strengthening our belief, the core principle behind our business mindset and psychology, we will tap into far more of our potential. In turn, this will facilitate more directed and focused actions, ultimately leading to greater results, leading to a higher degree of belief and certainty. This embodies the very momentum the name of this model eludes to.

With me so far? Okay, so you may be saying, "Well, that's all well and good, but *how* do I strengthen my belief?" I'm coming to that shortly – bear with me!

First, how do we know what results we want? Well, that's all part and parcel of creating a compelling vision. Time will always pass, no matter what we do. Yet we have a choice. We can either rock up haphazardly or we can plan and design our destiny purposefully, determining exactly what it is we want to aim for and change our actions in order to achieve these predetermined goals.

Sadly, I feel many of us go through life on autopilot and don't take the time to consider what it is we truly want to achieve. And that's where I am very passionate about helping people take time out and say, "Okay, let's consider what life you want." Whether that's personal or whether that's business, what are the *goals*? What are the objectives you want to aim for? Let's plan a strategy to design, purposefully, how to get there rather than just carry on on autopilot.

This will be much more powerful if I can encourage you to experience this rather than me just telling you. I will now provide you with a few simple instructions, and when I indicate, please put the book down and try this exercise for yourself.

First of all, stand up tall, feet together, facing forwards. Raise your right arm with your index finger pointing straight ahead. Without moving your feet, keep them pointed straight ahead, and I want you to turn as far as you comfortably can without hurting yourself or becoming unbalanced, and just notice how far you can turn, and then return to facing forward and lower your arm.

Next, as you are standing, close your eyes – without moving. I want you to *imagine* raising your arm in front of you with your index finger pointing ahead. Then, without actually moving, instead simply envisioning your action in your mind's eye, imagine yourself turning round. This time, however, imagine that you are turning twice as far effortlessly. Put a smile on your face, and just enjoy the experience, immersing yourself in your imagination – and have fun!

This may sound simple, but please repeat this exercise a couple more times as you imagine turning around a full 360 degrees, just like an owl, with fun and ease.

Now, the final step. Please open your eyes, and now raise your arm and see how far you can now actually turn around. Okay, all clear? Now, please put this book down and try the exercise.

Did you do it?

What were your results?

I bet I can guess because I have experienced this many times. Most people turn around at least 25% more after simply imagining turning around further in their mind for just 3 times. So, what is happening here? You see, we all have subconscious beliefs about everything in our lives, even about how far we can turn around! What this exercise demonstrates is how we can get results ahead of time in our minds to increase our level of belief and certainty. This allows us to tap into more of our potential and take greater action to ultimately achieve better results. What's more, we can employ this simple strategy in all areas of our life. Pretty cool, eh?

I wanted to demonstrate to you the importance of a strong sense of belief and certainty because, without these, the strategies I share with you will be of little value. Without these components, you will not have the motivation to implement these strategies.

> ***All power lies in execution.***

All great athletes know this, which is why they practice repetitively to master their craft and increase their level of certainty that they can perform at the highest level. This is no different for us as business entrepreneurs.

Have you ever been to a seminar or event where new information was delivered, yet once you came home, you simply re-immersed yourself into your daily life, criticizing yourself all the while for not taking action? Yes? Me too.

I've been very hard on myself at times, but the truth was that I implemented more than I gave myself credit for. What was wrong was the belief that I could hear something once, and because I understood it on an intellectual level, I thought I could immediately master it. My learning and development really started to take off when I *repeatedly* immersed myself in these materials and committed myself to mastery.

If you're committed to achieving outstanding results in your business, this will take *repetition, resolve* and *resilience* to keep going when the going gets tough and to ultimately achieve your desires, all of which can be applied to both business and life.

When we look at the most successful people in life, what do they all have in common? Well, I believe they have mastered this tool of momentum, learning how to increase their sense of certainty, partnering hunger and drive with a mission to create something extraordinary for both others and themselves.

We can't merely dabble if we want to create the success we desire. On an individual level, I cannot begin to describe how much I desire success for *you*. We *must* master this together.

Take a moment now to think about your achievements in life – how have you managed these? First, I believe we get obsessed about something, whereby it becomes so important to us, leaving nothing but determination to find a way to make it happen. We decide: *this is for me*! We keep thinking about it, driven to find answers, leaving us clear and obsessed.

Second, we start taking massive action. I believe it is better to take action, any action, than to sit and stew on something. Actions get us *moving*. Yet what do we do if our actions are not producing the results we want? Simply try something else. And if that doesn't work? Try something else again.

It is never too late to find new solutions to achieve even our most desirable results. We must simply continue with the process and persevere while staying resilient and resourceful. We can't hope that one solution will work and stop when it doesn't; we need to keep changing our actions until we do get what we desire. The key is simply to *get* moving and *keep* moving. What is the most important step in a journey of a thousand miles? The first one! So let's get going!

The best analogy I've heard about this process is asking a parent how long they will give their child to learn how to walk before saying, "Hey, just give it up; you're not a walker." I know it's crazy, right? No parent would say that. They would tell you, "My child will keep trying until they walk." This is why almost everyone can walk. If we can adopt this mindset to all our challenges, just think about the success we can achieve.

Now, the step of massive action can be sped up dramatically by adopting *effective execution*. We can't just 1. increase the output of our actions to keep running East, searching for a sunset. This simply won't work, no matter how positive we are. Now, we could 2. utilize trial and error, whereby we keep changing our approach until we find what works, but, as I wrote previously, that takes time. Or, we can 3. look for someone who has achieved success in what we want to achieve and model what they did to achieve it. I recommend option three.

I feel that most of us live our lives on autopilot. Yet we must remember that time flies really quickly. The next ten years will pass us by fleetingly; the question is, where will we be at the end of them? Will we turn up haphazardly, just doing what we have always done, or will we take time to design our destiny with purpose, planning, and creativity?

My mission in sharing this information with you is to condense decades of my learning and development and share it with you via a holistic and uniform resource that can be consumed in days, not years. To do so in order for you to learn both from my mistakes and my wins. For ultimately, my desire is for you to achieve success in all the areas of your life that are most important to you.

The first steps to take are to get obsessed with your desire – get clear on what it is that you want to achieve. Once you have a clear and compelling vision for what you want to achieve, commit to taking massive action toward the achievement of that goal. Building this mindset will then allow you to apply effective execution of the strategies I will share with you before culminating in the final step: grace. Some people call it luck, some call it God, and others grace. I believe in God, our Heavenly Father, and I believe God grants all our desires that we ask for in faith.

Now, my purpose is not at all to tell you what to believe, but have you ever noticed that there are times when you feel guided? That what occurred was due to more than just your efforts?

I believe the more we acknowledge the grace in our lives, the more grace we get to experience. Therefore, we merely need to practice these core principles in order to develop our core mission. To build our compelling vision for the future; to create our powerful reason why our goal is so important to us; to commit to taking massive action; to employ effective strategies; and to notice how grace shows up in our lives. If all of this can be achieved, then I truly believe anything is possible.

To bring this full circle, before I share with you further, I plead for you not to simply dabble in these materials. If you are truly ready to take your life and business to the next level, whatever that looks like for you, please commit fully to playing "full out" with me on our journey together. I believe there is power in simplicity, so I have deliberately designed this book with my most effective, simple tools and strategies. I encourage you to read through it several times and take notes.

An initial read-through will allow you to build a *cognitive* understanding. Further reads, along with taking notes and working through the exercises, will take this to the next level of *emotional* understanding. This will be where you start to feel so much emotion that you feel like you are moving, motivated for the new chapter in your life. This then leads to the final level of *physical* understanding, where you will ultimately take action and implement the strategies that I will share with you. I feel we don't truly *know* something until we are *doing* it consistently and until it becomes our new standard, part of our new identity.

If you are a business owner, or a fellow entrepreneur, I feel that we are like brothers and sisters, walking the same path. I am here to share all my passion, drive, and techniques to help you achieve both sustainable success and fulfillment in your business and life.

PART 1

SECTION TWO

The Triad – The 3 Molders of Meaning

> *Focus your energy on being the best you can be – the rest will work itself out.*
>
> *– Alex Parker*

In the last chapter, I talked about the Momentum Model and the importance of increasing our sense of belief and certainty to achieve our goals. In this chapter, I want to discuss the fuel that makes all this possible – our energy!

Energy is everything. Energy is life. Without energy, we die. It's that simple. I met with a client recently who sadly has been diagnosed with dementia. She's in a care home, and when I went to see her, she was sitting in a room all on her own. She looked so sad and alone. Within five minutes, she was laughing and chuckling with me because what I do is I bring energy to every situation. I was encouraging her to stand, to breathe, to smile, and there was such a difference in her – just like that.

This showed me that whatever our situation in life is, if we can bring energy to the situation, it's transformed. This is the power that positive energy can have in anyone's life. This frail old woman completely blossomed; she was smiling, and she was even laughing and blowing raspberries when I was teasing her and a little cheeky with her. It was just beautiful to see.

I wholeheartedly believe I was wasting my time, simply spinning my wheels, teaching my business strategies before I helped people with their energy, psychology, and mindset. It doesn't matter how powerful the strategies are, they will not be received, understood, and implemented unless the recipient is in an energetic state.

I know, myself, I cannot implement well unless I manage my energy first. I also know that the quickest way for me to change my energy is through my physiology. That's why I teach the Superman pose in every presentation I give, and I'll share it with you, too, later in this chapter. It is a powerful demonstration of how our energy can change dramatically, profoundly, and powerfully within just two minutes.

Most of us have a job, not a business, with the most strict employer that we've ever had. So we can't see the wood for the trees very often. As I said, I will share the Superman exercise with you a little later in this chapter, but briefly, it's been shown in a Harvard study that just standing in a strong pose, breathing firmly, with positive thoughts, within two minutes, changes our *biochemistry*. Now, that is amazing. It gives clarity of thought and all of these strong, energetic emotions. And you need a strong energy to follow through and implement, especially when challenges arise, as they invariably do.

It all comes down to energy. That's why I'm so passionate about this subject.

I want to credit Tony Robbins in this section as I share with you something that he refers to as the Triad of Emotional Psychology. This involves mastering the three forces that control our emotions, reflecting once again on the power of three.

I want to challenge you here to consider my belief that all of us do not experience life as some external force – we experience what we *focus on*. Have you heard the expression "information is power"? Well, I would change this to "information is *potential* power." EXECUTION trumps knowledge every time!

I make no apology for repeating my passion for execution because I truly want you to achieve *outstanding* results for your business ambitions and that, my friend, requires action and execution.

I want to spend some time sharing with you the tools to help you to take action and execute the strategies I will share later in this book.

Have you ever said to someone, "Oh yes, I know that," when they share some information with you? Well, my question to you is, are you *doing* it?!

Again, what I share comes from my own mistakes in life. I have often said this, "Yes, I know that," when I have attended many of my business conferences, but I had to admit that I wasn't doing it! I believe we only truly KNOW something when we DO it!

So, why is it that many of us say we *know* what to do but don't *do* it? This, my dear reader, is the essence of what I want to share with you in this section of my book. I want to help you not only understand the concepts that I share, but to put them into action consistently to realize your business goals – and I believe we need to generate high energy to lead to great execution.

I believe there are 3 questions we ask ourselves all the time or 3 decisions we are making all the time, consciously or subconsciously. These are:

1. What am I going to FOCUS on?
2. What does it MEAN?
3. What am I going to DO?

This highlights what I said before: that we do not experience life per se, we experience what we choose to focus on.

It is always useful to model those who excel in an area in which we wish to perform well. So, I want to credit Tony Robbins for what I share with you in this chapter. In my mind, Tony excels in so many areas, but especially on this topic of strengthening our mindset and learning how to generate energy, passion, and drive from within us to achieve our ambitions.

At one of his seminars, I remember Tony asking, what if we could make our worst day our best day? My first thought was, you don't know how bad my worst days are! However, after hearing Tony teach this so many times and reflecting on this for some time, I have begun to appreciate the great value in this teaching, and I can best demonstrate that through a story from my past.

Many years ago, I was deceived and defrauded in business, and I almost lost everything. I had bills to pay, payroll to meet, loan obligations to pay each month, and next to no income coming in; it was an immensely painful experience at the time. However, as I now look back on this experience, I can think of it as one of the best experiences in my life, not my worst. It led me to find powerful strategies to recover my position and it gave me amazing passion and drive to truly help and serve others at the highest level to save them from enduring what I went through, or at least provide them with shortcuts to expedite their recovery.

So, my question to you is – do you have a painful memory from your past, something you consider to be the worst day in your life? I think most of us do, but here is my next question that I want to ask you - how can you re-frame that experience to make it more empowering? Can you transform it into something that strengthened you and gave you new talents, determination, and drive that you would not have had if you had not had that experience?

I truly believe life happens FOR US, not TO US, and it can be immensely beneficial to re-frame past events to realize and appreciate the gifts that they gave us.

I believe all of us go to our "emotional home" under stress, and so I want to share with you ways in which I have learned to shore up and strengthen my emotional home. I want to introduce you to this concept of the Triad, three concepts being the Molders of Meaning.

The Triad is the foundation for life, for business, for whatever you want to achieve. It encompasses the power of three powerful components that can help you achieve whatever you set your mind to. Encompassing a strong Triad is like being reborn into a new experience. The best way I can describe it is reclaiming our God-given power, energy, and creative force.

The whole essence of the Triad is tapping into our innate energy; all of these aspects are helping towards that process. Why is that important? Because with energy, we can do anything and everything. Energy is the foundation of life, business, and our whole experience in this world.

With energy, we can achieve anything. Without energy, we're living a shadow of – a fraction of – what is possible. It brings ideas or concepts into reality. It's the power or the juice to drive us forward.

Each element in the Triad works together for harmony and brings a powerful effect to your results. You can make dramatic changes in your experience and power by shifting just one of the three elements, but by bringing the three together, the whole is greater than the sum of the parts. Let's examine the parts.

Physiology
What does physiology mean in the context of the Triad? Of the three parts, this is the most powerful and quickest way to change our emotional state. It is what we do with our body – how we breathe, stand, move. This affects the energy that we can summon, at any moment, within us to achieve our objectives. Just the concept of breathing correctly gives you access to energy reserves that you may not even realize you have – up until now.

Focus
So then, what is focusing in the context of the Triad? Focus is simply what we give our attention to, purposely, passionately, with energy. Where we concentrate our attention determines what happens. It actually creates different experiences. If we give our attention to something we're confident in, something that's empowering, it's

energizing. Whereas if we focus on our limitations or challenges, that can be disempowering.

Focus is something that I am very passionate about in my work; I'm very focused to achieve the outcomes that I set for myself. I focus on one thing, see it through to fruition, and then move to another project. That focused attention allows me to achieve whatever I must.

When I had my previous business, I had a team of six people. I had to let go of the tax manager. At the time, I had a practice where I had 300 tax returns. So I took on responsibility for doing that as well as my managerial role whilst I had a gap before I could refill the position. When the new employee started, he couldn't believe that I had completed 300 tax returns single-handedly, without any support and without any mistakes. That, I believe, is a result of my focused attention to the task at hand and seeing it through to the outcome that I had envisioned.

Language and Meaning
What do language and meaning mean in the context of the Triad? I'm a man of faith. The Bible starts by saying God said, "Let there be light," and there was light. I believe we are created in the image and likeness of God, and therefore we have the same creative power. Our words are one of the ways in which we have that creative power. So I'm very mindful of the words and the language that I choose, as well as the meaning I give to my words. Sometimes I'll backtrack and say, "Cancel that. Let me rephrase that," because I truly

believe there's so much power in the words that we choose to articulate our thoughts and ideas. When it comes to what we wish to convey to ourselves and to others, words are so powerful. Why are they important? Because they change our experience for us and for those that we interact with.

Here's an impactful example of shifting language to shift meaning.

I believe in moments of challenge, we all have a question that we repeatedly ask ourselves. My old pattern when going through a very challenging time in life was when I used to ask myself, "Why is this happening to me?" I have since changed that to when I go through challenges, I ask myself, "What can I learn from this? What's the benefit of this?" That's such a more empowering use of language, and that immediately shifts my energy from a disempowered state to an empowered state. I have the energy to call upon to create something new.

Now it's time to play with creating a Triad for yourself!

Please take a blank page in your notes and draw a triangle. In the center of this triangle, write EMOTIONAL STATE. Then underneath the triangle, please write 1. PHYSIOLOGY – and all I mean by physiology is how we move our bodies. On the left-hand side of the triangle, please write 2. FOCUS. And on the right-hand side of the triangle, write 3. LANGUAGE/MEANING. Above the triangle, please write 4. CREATE A COMPELLING FUTURE, and then underneath the triangle, please write 5. IDENTITY. This is shown in "The Triad" image below, and I encourage you to draw this out in your notes. This reflects the three forces that control our emotional psychology – our physiology, focus, and language, and these are the forces we can employ to create a compelling future and a strong and empowering identity.

THE TRIAD

4. CREATE A COMPELLING FUTURE
A powerful WHY is the fuel to use our skills

2. FOCUS – Where focus goes, energy flows

3. LANGUAGE/MEANING – Emotion = Life

EMOTIONAL STATE

1. PHYSIOLOGY
How we move our body
Our Foundation

5. IDENTITY
We don't do what we can
We live our lives in accordance with who we believe we are

By far, the most important of these is our physiology – how we move our body. Just think about how we hold and move our body when we feel happy, cheerful, or powerful? Well, we stand tall and smile while our shoulders are relaxed. Our chest will often be out as we breathe deeply in a calm and relaxed way. So, how do we hold our bodies when we feel unsure, fearful, or sad, on the other hand? Well, we tend to hunch our shoulders, holding tension within our bodies, while our breath is shallow.

Numerous scientific studies have shown if we hold and move our body in the ways we naturally do when we feel good, we can influence our emotional state. And rather than just tell you the science, it is perhaps much more powerful to demonstrate this to you.

Let's participate in the following exercise together, so I can share with you an important lesson I have learned, one which helps me all the time with both my own psychology and those of the clients I teach.

Please indulge me for just two minutes – I won't keep you any longer! Please stand up, and adopt what I call the Superman or Superwoman pose. Stand tall, feet apart, hands on hips, shoulders back, and chest out. Breathe deeply through your diaphragm, and most importantly, smile and have fun with this.

Stand powerfully in this pose for just two minutes while I explain the science behind this.

Research has been undertaken at Harvard University, showing that just standing powerfully like this for a mere two minutes changes our biochemistry! The hormone testosterone, which is important for both men and women, increases by about 35%, and cortisol, the stress hormone, reduces by about the same amount. This results in greater clarity of thought, more confidence, and the willingness to take more risks – all from just standing powerfully for two minutes. What's more, the effects of this can be greatly increased by adding movement. I like to add jumping jacks or press-ups to increase my energy levels, which is very important for me since I sit a lot at my job.

So, did you do the exercise? How do you feel after just two minutes? It's powerful, isn't it?

Not only is this a powerful bio-hack that we can use at any time, but we can also share this with our team to re-energize them, all the while demonstrating the power of physiology on our well-being and emotional psychology.

I have learned how to demand more energy from myself. I live a very healthy lifestyle, with fasting, good nutrition, and exercise. Yet, by far, the greatest tool I have for increasing and sustaining my energy levels is an understanding of the Triad of Emotional Psychology and knowing that a quick change in my physiology can produce immediate access to increased levels of energy.

The second force in the Triad is Focus. What we focus on is very powerful and impacts our mindset. For instance, are we focused on what we have or what we want? What we are grateful for, or what we are frustrated about? Are we focused on the present, past, or future? What we can control, or what we can't?

> *Our past does not control our future unless we live there!*
>
> – Tony Robbins

What we choose to focus on has a massive effect on our psychology and well-being.

There are 3 patterns of focus, showing once more the power of 3. Please think for a moment; do you mostly focus on:

1. What is missing or what you have and are grateful for?

2. What you can control or what you can't control?

3. Where is your focus the most – the past, the present, or the future?

I hope you will see that where we place our focus very much affects our emotions and, therefore, our energy levels. For example, if we mostly focus on what is missing, we could feel feelings of fear or anger rather than focusing on what we have and enjoying a sense of peace and gratitude. Although, a focus on what is missing can sometimes provide us with the drive and determination to achieve new things if we channel this energy in positive ways.

Again, I want to share a lesson from my mistakes. One thing I have been bad at in the past is not celebrating my little wins along the way. I find there are 3 powerful words that I now use to create new opportunities for me, and these are "up until now."

If I say, "Up until now, I have been bad at not celebrating my wins and immersing myself in the powerful energies of celebration along my path," this immediately opens up the opportunity for positive changes *from now on*.

So, if you ever catch yourself telling someone about any weaknesses or shortcomings, please adopt the phrase "up until now" and just watch how your emotions and energy change with this powerful 3-word phrase, which leads me nicely on to the third force in the Triad: language and meaning.

The language we use, and the meaning we give it, makes a massive difference to our experience. So, we need to ensure that our language is empowering, not disempowering.

We ought to practice an awareness of our language. If we notice our language is disempowering, just notice this, celebrate our awareness, and change this to be more empowering. Words impact our lives. For example, people often say, "I *have* to do this or that." If we change the statement to "I *get* to do this," just feel the energy inside of yourself change with that slight tweak of language. Just by changing one word, we can powerfully and profoundly change our lives.

I strive to adopt the 90-second rule. If we notice we feel angry or frustrated, by all means, vent and express it. But within 90 seconds, we can practice calming down. We can then change our focus, our language, and our physiology to a more empowered state of being. It's okay to get upset and frustrated; it's not okay to stay there!

> *Remember, nothing has any meaning except the meaning we give it.*

I don't know what motivated you to choose to read this book. I'm guessing you want to make some positive changes. I'm just delighted that you are here, and I have an opportunity to share with you powerful techniques that I have learned throughout my career. So I'd like to take this moment to share with you three powerful forces to creating lasting change:

1. FOCUS
2. MASSIVE ACTION
3. GRACE

Focus provides the power of absolute clarity and commitment, and if we follow this up with massive action, not just dabbling, but massive, consistent, and effective action, then I believe there is only the last component of grace that is required to achieve anything. I'm not here to tell you what to believe; for my part, I believe in God, my Heavenly

Father, who watches over me and guides me to achieve my desires. You might substitute this for the Universe, luck, or destiny, but my point is this, have you ever noticed the harder you work at something, the luckier you become?

Jim Rohn used to teach *Success Leaves Clues*. I believe there is great power in finding someone who is achieving success in an area you wish to excel in and model what they do to emulate their success. This way, the action we take can be effective execution rather than trial and error.

I also want to share my belief that what we GET will never bring us happiness; who we BECOME has the power to make us happy or unhappy.

I believe there are two master skills in business and in life:

1. The SCIENCE of Achievement

AND

2. The ART of Fulfillment

I say the science of achievement because I believe with the right strategy, hard work, and dedication, we can ACHIEVE anything we set our heart and minds to, but *fulfillment* is an art! I believe the ultimate failure is to achieve success without fulfillment, and I believe the secret to fulfillment comes from our GROWTH and CONTRIBUTION. I said earlier what we get will never make us happy; it's who we become that has the power to make us happy and fulfilled.

I want so much to help you achieve all the success you desire for your business, and I believe by giving you a solid foundation in what I have learned about psychology and energy, I can help you achieve your wildest visions for your business. But I also want so much for you to feel happy and fulfilled in attaining all that you set out to achieve on our journey together.

It's in our *decisions* that our destiny is shaped, which is why I chose the tagline of *Destiny By Design*™ for my strategic coaching business, and our destiny is as much about who we become, not just what we achieve.

Ultimately, I believe we need to be resourceful. If you ask anyone why they have not achieved what they want, often they will talk about a lack of time, a lack of skills, and a lack of resources. However, I believe the ultimate resource is resourcefulness, and this comes from the energy we can summon at will to achieve our ambitions in life, which is why I have taken some time to share and go through the Triad and the 3 Moulders of Meaning with you.

For your **Complimentary Financial Statement Demonstration** 5-Part video series to accompany the mastery steps in this book, while available, visit www.AlexParker.UK.com

PART 1

SECTION THREE

Three Foundational Principles of Business

> *We are all equal as human beings, but we are not all equal in the marketplace.*
>
> *– Jim Rohn*

How can a business set itself apart from its competitors? I'm passionate about helping and serving my clients. We ought to work with our clients at the highest possible level.

I remember at a business event put on by Tony Robbins, he talked about the different levels of service.

He was describing that if, historically, we provided poor service, we're going to get poor results. And there's a big, big, big leap up from poor to good.

And historically, if we provided a good service, we would receive good results.

But the marketplace today is so competitive that if we now strive to provide a good service, what do you feel the results will be? Most people would expect us to get good results for a good service, but it's not. We get poor results because of the level of competition.

So the next level up is, again, a massive leap from 'good' to 'excellent.' And a lot of business entrepreneurs are striving for excellence, with the expectation that they will achieve excellent results. But again, because of the competitive marketplace we're all operating in now, our rewards for offering an excellent service will only be *good*. This means *pain* because our expectations are not being met.

My desire is to share with you that there's another level over 'excellent.' You might say to me, "But I'm giving everything I have to achieve 'excellence.' I don't have any more." But there's always another level.

Here's the good news …

The difference from 'excellent' to the next level, which is 'outstanding,' is merely a 2mm shift! And the reward for that extra step to the 'outstanding' level is exponential.

> **This is how you set your business apart from your competitors – *be outstanding.***

I believe the philosophy that drives sustainable business growth is to always add more value. The best way I have found to start this journey is with what I refer to as the 3 Foundational Principles of Business:

1. Know our ideal client – what do they want most? What do they need most? What do they fear most?

2. Create an irresistible offer – create an offer that has them thinking, "It's just a no-brainer to say yes to working with you."

3. Over-deliver – deliver more value than our customers ever expect to receive.

I learned this from a business event delivered by Tony Robbins. I have found this to be extremely powerful, so I am delighted to have the opportunity to share it with you.

To begin, I will tackle the first, outlining what it means to know your ideal client and the importance of doing so. Lots of marketing people often talk about "client avatars," but what does that really mean? For me, that means getting inside the head of our clients or *potential* clients and knowing exactly what they're thinking.

Being absolutely clear on who your client avatar is matters toward your success.

To truly understand our client will accelerate your business:
- What is it they want?
- What is it that they need?
- What are they fearful of?
- What is the burning problem that we solve for them?
- What's the outcome that they desire from us?

The client avatar is the details or makeup of your ideal client, such as:
- Where do they live?
- What's the makeup of their family?
- What's their income?
- What is their education level?
- What hobbies do they enjoy?

Have a vision of a singular client who is an ideal client that you serve – that is your Avatar. Combining these elements, our intention must always be to realize exactly what the problem is that we are going to solve for our client. Oftentimes, as business owners, we get so passionate about our product or our service. But clients don't buy *products* or *services*. They buy *results*. They buy *outcomes*.

It is our responsibility to know exactly what it is our clients want and need. Therefore, we can tailor our offer to meet those very wants and needs head-on. It is no good having a great product or service if it's not something our clients and customers actually want.

Yet, what if you don't have an ideal client? How can you figure out exactly who to target?

When you design your marketing activities, it's important to have in mind serving the one ideal client and not a multitude of clients because then it will attract the ideal client to work with. Just as importantly, we will also repel those people that aren't our ideal client so we don't waste our time or theirs. Time is our most precious resource. This allows us to be fully committed to those who are ready to receive our outstanding service and not be distracted by time wasters.

I have met so many people who simply believe a client is a client, no matter what. Well, we can all get customers and clients, but what we really want are *raving fans*. Nowadays, it is not enough in the wildly competitive business world, regardless of industry, to merely have financial interactions between customers and your business. Word-of-mouth marketing, leading to both customer retention and referrals, is one of the keys to achieving *long-term* financial success. And knowing your ideal client is the first place to start in order to understand exactly how we are going to provide this service and achieve this success.

Working in the accounting industry, I have always said that I am in the relationship business first and the accounting business second. It is these very relationships that I built with my clients that made my business as successful as it is.

To nurture these relationships, we need to tailor our offer to meet our client's needs and desires. For if we don't, they are not going to stay our clients for very long. They will go out and look for someone else who *will* meet their criteria. So in order to provide this level of service and create sustainable relationships, we first need to understand the wants and needs of our ideal client.

The second step is to create an irresistible offer. But what separates the irresistible offers from the generic?

Well, we are all bombarded with offers every day of the week, whether in storefronts or adverts that pop up on our devices. But despite seeing hundreds of advertisements a day, we never follow all of them up – how could we? So much mediocrity riddles the marketplace, and it is left to us to decide what we wish to engage with. Yet, every now and again, an offer comes along that immediately grabs our attention and seemingly forces us to purchase it.

It is this very sensation that we need to create for our clients. We want our clients, when they receive our offer, to say, "Wow, of course, I want to do business with this company. Why wouldn't I?" It might seem impossible right now, but fortunately, there are many different ways you can achieve this.

Some of the most important of these, I have found, include:

- Product and service bundles
- Risk reversal

- Guarantees

Product and Service Bundles

My personal preference is the first of these, bundling different products and services together to increase the value proposition. In order to do this, one effective technique is to look in the marketplace and see who's doing this best within your own industry. Take Apple, for example. If, for instance, you want an Apple iPhone, you may start by going on the Apple website. Yet once you arrive, there isn't just one phone that you add to your basket and move on your way. No, instead, there is a multitude of choices with variations of size, color, memory, and functionality. What's more, you are also presented with the option for additional products, such as a case, screen cover, and insurance, for a reduced price when selected with the only thing you originally thought you were coming for: the phone.

There are so many different items that are bundled together to make it a more attractive proposition, and we can apply this very approach to our own businesses to create that irresistible offer. One where the client says, "Oh, yes, of course, I'll do business with you." Because why wouldn't they, right?

Importantly, this approach provides your customers with a sense of choice. In my own business, I used to create a proposal for accounting services and I simply said, "This is what we do; would you like it?" Yet, when I changed to offer a choice (a gold, silver, and bronze service), my proposal shifted to informing my clients that they had the option of three different levels of service. By providing this sense of choice, you can immediately engage in a conversation with the client far easier than when providing them with a binary option. Saying, "This is what we do. Do you want it?" is a mere yes or no answer. But if we ask, "Which one would suit you best?" the conversation continues. This, ultimately, is a far more powerful question by offering this notion of choice. Certainly, in my experience, the conversion rate was dramatically higher when I made this small tweak.

Risk Reversal

Risk reversal is a strategy to consider when creating an irresistible offer. We should think about how we can reduce friction wherever possible for the client and risk reversal gives reassurance. If there's any hesitation in the mind of our prospect, risk reversal means we, as the vendor, take on the risk. Remove the risk from the client, reduce the friction, and make it easier for the client to say yes.

An example of risk reversal is having a money-back guarantee. Or you could have a guarantee within a service contract, like much of my work. If the contract is for a certain period of time, say six months, the risk reversal could state that we will continue to work with you for up to 12 months to ensure we meet the objective. There are many ways to reverse the risk. Just a word of caution though – if we make promises to work for an extended period to deliver a certain outcome, we need to set out what we require from our customers to play their part in the agreement.

Guarantees

A guarantee and risk reversal are quite closely linked. A guarantee is a promise that a certain objective will be met.

This assurance is twofold: it gives customers reassurance but also value for us because we do not want to work with customers who cannot see the value. Consider how best to expand on this concept.

A guarantee works both ways because if we're going to make a promise of risk reversal in achieving a certain outcome or result for our client, then we must ask them to commit to playing their part. If a client isn't willing to make that level of commitment, then they're not the right client for us. We have to be very selective and discerning in our choice of who we work with.

Irresistible Offer

It's so important to have an irresistible offer. It reduces friction in the sale, making it as easy as possible, compelling people to say yes.

Let me give you an example. I had a client for whom I was providing basic accounting and tax services. He was struggling with his book-keeping and looking for a solution. But before I knew about that, he contacted me saying, " I really value the service that you provide, I love what you stand for, how you've helped in the past, and gone above and beyond my expectations, but the one thing you don't provide is book-keeping services, so I found somebody that will do book-keeping services and accounting." I asked this client if I could produce an offer that would include a solution for his book-keeping, "Would you allow me to present that to you and consider it?" And he said, "Yes, of course, because we have a strong relationship." So I created a relationship with another company to produce a back office team so that I could go into the marketplace with an offer for book-keeping services as well as my accounting services.

I came to him with a bundled offer, which included book-keeping. The irresistible offer came in the way I structured it – the price point was almost identical to what he was already getting from me without the additional expense of the external book-keeper. I said, "You can have everything you've previously had, plus the addition of a book-keeping service with monthly figures. We can touch base on a much more frequent basis with reliable figures from which we can make managerial, strategic decisions." He said, "It's a no-brainer; of course, I accept! I will tell the other company I will stay with you." That, to me, is the power of an irresistible offer.

The final Foundational Principle of Business is to over-deliver. If we are able to give more than our clients could ever expect to receive, this will, in turn, build a strong, trusted, and reliable business reputation. When we do this *consistently*, we can then create a brand, leading to even greater business acceleration and growth.

Now, some of my business strategy clients have often been tentative when it comes to this idea of over-deliverance. They seem to think that it merely means giving products and services away for less money, leading to both a waste of their own time and resources.

These are interesting concerns, and at least on a surface level, I can understand the trepidation displayed by these clients. However, in business, I believe we must inherently realize that we should not wait for the exchange of money before we add value. Instead, we should assume that everyone we talk to will eventually become a client. Therefore, we should start adding value at the very first interaction to start building trust in our relationship. This, in turn, will allow us to create a good reputation and, in time, solidify a trustworthy brand.

Creating a respected brand is a powerful tool in business – for example, people will reach past all other drinks in a display to choose a Coca-Cola, and they will pay far more for a Mercedes car, a Nike sportswear, or a Louis Vuitton bag because these companies have worked hard to create their well-recognized, valued brands.

The way *we* can start to achieve this is to over-deliver.

Too often, businesses do not even think about this; instead, they merely rely on one original, and at times basic, value proposition. Indeed, it is just the top few percent of businesses that do successfully over-deliver. Yet the rewards for doing so far outweigh the effort required to carry this out. I believe it is the right thing to do when acting both in the interests of yourself and your client, but also ties into commercially sound business strategy, as well.

To give a real-world example of these 3 Foundational Principles in action, I want to share with you the story of Tony Hsieh, who used this to great effect with Zappos Shoes. I have heard this story told many times at Tony Robbins' business events, and I am pleased I can now share this story with a wider audience.

Zappos Shoes had a business selling shoes on the internet just prior to the year 2000, and they were in trouble. The business was not looking good; in fact, they were quickly running out of cash and facing bankruptcy, so they were looking for investors to survive. Now, do you remember what was happening as we approached the year 2000? I do. There was a great concern that all computers would stop working as the year changed from 1999 to 2000, and this would cause a great disruption to business, to put it mildly. So business owners were having great difficulty in finding investment for their businesses.

Now enter Tony Hsieh. Tony saw an opportunity based on the 3 Foundational Principles of Business I shared earlier. He saw this business already had their ideal client – women! We all know women, and some men, but mainly women, have a very special relationship when it comes to shoes. They buy shoes in all manner of shapes, sizes, colors, and styles. They have different shoes for different occasions, and some women will even buy shoes that do not fit because they like them so much and hope that someday they will fit! :-)

So he said to this business, you already have your ideal client; you now need an irresistible offer. The business model before Tony came along was that the customer would choose their shoes and pay to ship the shoes to them, and then if they didn't like them, they had to pay to ship them back for a refund. Tony suggested that they change their offer – the new offer should be: buy as many shoes as you want, and *we* will pay to ship these to you, and if you do not like any of them, *we* will pay to ship them back to us, no questions asked. The business owners said, "We can't do that; we will go bankrupt." But Tony said, "You're already going bankrupt; you need to try something new." And the rest, as they say, is history!

Over the next few years, business accelerated. Tony instilled a business culture of over-deliverance to build a strong reputation and brand. His motto was that Zappos Shoes' mission was to make their customers happy. He knew he had achieved this when he was at a party one night, and one of the ladies there was very drunk and started shouting that she wanted a pizza. It was past midnight and the staff at the event told her it was late and they could not help her, so she announced loudly that she would call her Zappos representative!

Tony listened attentively to what happened next. The lady got through to her Zappos representative and announced loudly that she wanted a pepperoni pizza. The representative at the other end of the phone replied, "Ma'am, we are Zappos Shoes; we don't sell pizzas," but the lady said, "I know that, but you're meant to make me happy!"

Tony thought, "This should be interesting." The Zappos representative asked the lady to hold on a minute and then returned shortly and said, "Of course, Ma'am, tell me what you need!" The lady asked who else wanted pizza, and shortly afterward, half a dozen pizzas arrived to satisfy this lady's request. It was at that moment that Tony realized he had instilled a culture of over-deliverance into his company. Their mission was to make their customers happy and they were committed to doing whatever it took to achieve this.

Zappos Shoes was sold to Amazon in 2009 for $1.2 Billion and I believe Tony remained on as CEO until he sadly passed in 2020. Now, this is the most powerful real-world story I have heard about these 3 Foundational Principles of Business in action, and I am overjoyed to share this with you because I believe these stories are great teachings for all of us.

My belief is we all want our clients to be raving fans. We want them to be so enthused and delighted with the outcome we deliver that they will tell everybody that they know about our wonderful outstanding service. How can businesses over-deliver for their clients? Over-delivery is just simply producing a result in giving a service, adding far more value than our customers ever expect to receive.

In business, the value proposition means there's a cost of delivery and there's an outcome delivered for the client. If the client perceives that the outcome delivered is demonstrably higher than the level of investment required, this is where we succeed in over-delivery.

A great example of over-delivering, from my own experience, is when I had a Tesla Powerwall battery fitted in my house. A client of mine saw that I had solar panels on my roof and suggested having a battery pack to store that energy. I ordered a battery pack and I explained to the company that my overriding outcome was I wanted to be energy independent in the event of a power cut. I wanted a system that the battery would take over the moment the power outage happened. And so they fitted this battery bank. On completion of the fitting, I asked them to tell me how it works with taking over in the event of a power outage. The installer said to me, "Oh, this system doesn't produce that outcome. For that, you need a Tesla Powerwall."

So I went back to the salesperson, reminding him that I specifically said I wanted this result. He replied, "I'm so sorry. Yes, you do need a Tesla Powerball to achieve your desired outcome and it's double the level of investment, but it's our mistake. We'll take out what we put in at no charge, and we'll deliver you the Tesla Powerwall that gives you the result we promised at no extra charge." They explained there would be a delay in securing the product. They couldn't have done more as they bent over backward in touching base with me and keeping me informed. They prioritized the delivery of the unit. And they tested it afterward to make sure it worked. The end result was I had exactly the product that I'd asked for, giving me the result that I wanted at no extra fee. That, to me, was an example of setting a standard of over-delivery.

PART 2
HOW TO UNDERSTAND AND READ FINANCIAL STATEMENTS

*Understanding your own
financial statements is such
an integral part of understanding
your own business and industry
in order to build and sustain success.
I will empower you to learn
how to read these statements,
then understand where
and how to employ little tweaks
that will improve your business,
along with simple tools that will enable
positive financial change.*

PART 2

SECTION ONE

Seeing Beyond
The Balance Sheet

> *If you can't read the scoreboard,*
> *you don't know the score.*
> *If you don't know the score,*
> *you can't tell the winners from the losers.*
> *– Warren Buffett*

I believe most business owners are very good at their business but not so good at the financial side of it. They will often wait until after the end of the year, when their accountant will produce their financial statements, normally six months, or more, later with figures that are then out of date, to be told how well or otherwise their business performance has been. Yet what most businesses fail to understand is that they need their financial information on a *monthly* basis.

At the same time, most people simply get their accounts done to calculate the tax. They do not, however, realize that there is a storehouse of value within every figure, often left ignored, to help them navigate the waters of their business.

I remember so well when I first qualified as an accountant and became more client-facing. I would work so hard to produce what I felt to be the best possible financial statements I could: the most accurate, the most detailed, the most professionally presented. But most clients did not seem to appreciate all my hard work, they just asked, "Where do I sign and how much tax do I have to pay?"

Another set of questions I am often asked is, "How much money have I made?" and "Where has it all gone?"

I believe we all want to do well in business so we can do well in our lives, take care of our families, and contribute to our wider community. I think it was Einstein that said "Compound interest is the eighth wonder of the world – he who understands this earns it, and he who doesn't understand this, pays it!" I also love a quote I heard from Keith Cunningham; he said, "Success is getting what you want. Fulfillment is giving what you got."

All this leads me to share with you that sometimes we don't need more wins; sometimes we just need to stop making so many mistakes in our business – and the way we achieve this, I believe, starts with better understanding our numbers!

The analogy I often like to make is to compare business owners with pilots, and this is why I changed my business website to include a photo of a plane. As business owners, the vast majority of us are flying with only one dial – revenue! As I mentioned earlier, in our business cockpit, we have a huge array of dials (financial measurements) to indicate where we are now, and we have various levers (strategies) to take us to where we want to go. But the vast majority of us, and I include myself in this because I did this before I learned these important lessons, are driving our business blindfolded. Here's another way to think about it, how far would we get if we tried to drive our car blindfolded?

I believe we need to keep asking ourselves, what can I do today to improve my situation? I don't need to be perfect; I just need to start on a path of constant and never-ending improvement. And to do this, the first step, I believe, is we need to learn how to keep score.

If I were to look at a cricket scoreboard or a baseball scoreboard, I would not have a clue what this information was telling me. I don't know how to keep score, but if you show me a tennis scoreboard, I know in an instant who is playing, what the score is, who is winning, how close we are to the end of the game, etc. We need a scoreboard to tell us the results. All games have a language; if we do not know the language, we can't play the game – and the language of business is accounting! I believe it was Warren Buffet who said this.

What I am about to share in this section on how to understand and read financial statements I learned from Keith Cunningham, someone who I have found deeply inspirational. He started his presentation by saying he would teach us the equivalent of 2 years of Harvard accounting in about an hour – all without ever mentioning debits and credits! As an accountant, I thought, "This should be interesting, he was planning on doing the impossible," but he did not disappoint, and I have taught this in the way I learned from Keith ever since.

As accountants, essentially, we convert activities to numbers. Think of a set of bathroom scales, you jump on the scales, and it shows you a measurement, but what if we can reverse engineer our results to learn how we can change our activities to achieve different results? This section is all about creating better optics to make better decisions, make more money, and make fewer assumptions. The first step to achieving this, in my opinion, is to gain a basic understanding of reading our financial statements.

Please don't misunderstand me; I do not want to teach you to become an accountant. That is not the highest and best use of your time.

> *I want to teach you to read the optics in your business.*

So let's start by discussing the first dial in our business cockpit, the first report card prepared by our accountants.

I encourage you to please participate fully with me in this section by drawing out the diagrams I describe. Scientific research shows that by taking notes when learning something new, our retention is significantly improved compared to when we just listen passively. So please join in by drawing all the diagrams I am describing in this section because this will really help your understanding of these concepts, which will help you when I share my strategies in the next section.

So first, please draw out a square in your notes. Divide that square into two equal parts with a vertical line through the middle, and then divide the right half of the square again into two equal parts with a horizontal line, as shown in the image below:

Now let's start by adding some details. At the top of the large left-hand rectangle, write the heading: "Things and Stuff". At the top of the top right-hand square, write the heading: "Owe". And at the top of the lower right-hand square, please write the heading: "Own". This is shown on the next image:

THINGS & STUFF	OWE
	OWN

This report card has 3 basic parts; this measures the Things and Stuff of a business, what the business Owes, and what a business Owns.

Things and stuff a business owns will include Property, Plant, and Equipment (PPE), monies owed from customers, Accounts Receivable (A/R), Stock or Inventory of goods, and Cash.

A business will owe monies owed to its suppliers, Accounts Payable (A/P), Taxes owed to the government, Taxes Payable (T/P), and amounts owed on its loans, Loans Payable (L/P).

A business owns the initial investment made by the owner, the shareholders, and its profits or earnings.

So before we go any further, please let me just expand a little on these terms to make sure I convey these details to you in an understandable form. A business may buy a property to work from, or a piece of equipment to produce products, or indeed may buy a vehicle to transport the owner or stock. A business will buy these "things and stuff" in order to generate income/revenue for the business – more on this later.

If a business buys products to sell, or indeed makes products to sell, more than likely, it will not sell all of these goods at once. The goods awaiting sale are called **stock or inventory.**

When a business makes a sale, often our customers will not necessarily pay us straight away; they will essentially give us an I.O.U. instead and pay later, say within 30 days. While we wait for our invoice to be paid, this debt is called an **Accounts Receivable**.

The opposite of an Accounts Receivable is an Accounts Payable. When we buy something from a supplier, often we will not have to pay for this straight away; we are given a period of credit, like an I.O.U. Until we pay this debt, this is called an **Accounts Payable**.

When we make sales, we will usually have to make payment of a Sales Tax to our respective government, or when we make profits, we will need to make a tax payment based on our profits, but usually, we are given some time before we need to make these payments. Whilst these payments remain due to the government, these are called **Taxes Payable**.

If we take out finance for the business, we will normally negotiate a term of repayment for our loan. Until we make our final repayment on our loan, we will have an amount due to be repaid to our lender. We call this amount a **Loan Payable**.

Okay, now I have explained these terms, let's now add these details to our diagram. In the left-hand rectangle under the heading we wrote for Things and Stuff, let's now write: **PPE (Plant, Property, and Equipment)**, **A/R (Accounts Receivable)**, **Stock or Inventory**, and **Cash**. In the higher right-hand square, under our heading of Owe, let's write: A/P (Accounts Payable), T/P (Taxes Payable), and L/P (Loans Payable). In the lower right-hand square under our heading Own, let's now write Owner's Investment and Profits/Earnings. This is now shown on the next image:

THINGS & STUFF	**OWE**
PPE	A/P
A/R	T/P
STOCK / INVENTORY	L/P
CASH	
	OWN
	OWNER'S INVESTMENT
	PROFIT / EARNINGS

Now, the left-hand side of our report card will equal the right-hand side. Things and Stuff will equal what we owe plus what we own, so that the left-hand side balances with the right-hand side. This is why accountants call this report card a **Balance Sheet.**

Think of this as a PHOTOGRAPH, a SNAPSHOT, a moment in time as though we have taken a photograph of the business, so you will see that this report card will show a title of Balance Sheet as at … a certain date – 31 March, 30 June, 31 December, for example. At this date, this is the measurement of Things and Stuff, what the business owes and what the business owns.

Now accountants call Things and Stuff – **Assets**, what a business owes – **Liabilities**, and what a business owns – **Equity, Reserves**, or **Capital**. So let's add this information to our diagram. Let's write a heading of "**Assets**" where we previously wrote Things and Stuff, "**Liabilities**" where we previously wrote Owe, and "**Equity/Reserves/Capital,**" where we previously wrote Own, and let's add a heading at the top of our diagram saying BALANCE SHEET AS AT on the next image:

BALANCE SHEET AS AT....

ASSETS (Things & Stuff)	**LIABILITIES** (Owe)
PLANT	ACCOUNTS PAYABLE
PROPERTY	TAXES PAYABLE
EQUIPMENT	LOANS PAYABLE
ACCOUNTS RECIEVABLE	
STOCK / INVENTORY	
CASH	
	EQUITY / RESERVES / CAPITAL (Own)
	SHARE CAPITAL
	PROFITS / EARNINGS

Nowadays, here in the UK, at least, the Balance Sheet is often shown in vertical format rather than horizontally, so let me help you draw this diagram. Please take a fresh piece of paper and draw a rectangle down the page. Now draw a horizontal line splitting the rectangle ⅔ to ⅓ with the smaller ⅓ are at the bottom. Please see the next image:

Now, let's enter our headings. At the top of the rectangle, let's write, "Assets (Things and Stuff)", half-way down, the top rectangle, let's write "Liabilities (Owe)", and then in the lower rectangle, let's write a heading of "Capital/Equity (Own)". Please see image below:

ASSETS *(Things & Stuff)*

LIABILITIES *(Owe)*

CAPITAL/EQUITY *(Own)*

And finally, let's enter our details from our earlier horizontal diagram. So under Assets, we will write PPE (Plant, Property, and Equipment), A/R (Accounts Receivable), Stock or Inventory, and Cash. Under our heading of Liabilities, let's write: A/P (Accounts Payable), T/P (Taxes Payable), and L/P (Loans Payable), and in the lower rectangle under our heading of Capital/Equity, let's now write Owner's Investment and Profits/Earnings. This is now shown on the next image:

BALANCE SHEET AS AT....

ASSETS *(Things & Stuff)*
PPE (Plant, Property, and Equipment)
A/R (Accounts Receivable)
Stock or Inventory
Cash

LIABILITIES *(Owe)*
A/P (Accounts Payable)
T/P (Taxes Payable)
L/P (Loans Payable)

CAPITAL/EQUITY *(Own)*
Owner's Investment
Profits/Earnings

So you now have drawn both types of Balance Sheets you will see accountants prepare, both the horizontal format and the vertical format. This is the first report card. Now, let me tell you about the second report card accountants will prepare for a business …

PART 2

SECTION TWO

Make a Statement

Through Your Income Statements

> *I don't need to do more smart things.*
> *I just need to do fewer dumb things.*
> — Keith Cunningham

Now it's time for me to introduce you to the second report card that accountants prepare. Please take a fresh piece of paper and draw a rectangle down the page, and just as we did for the vertical Balance Sheet, please draw a horizontal line about ⅔ down the rectangle. This is shown on the next image:

This report card measures Sales – referred to as **Sales, Revenue, or Turnover**. From this, we deduct the business expenses to arrive at The Bottom Line, which we call **Net Income, Profits, or Earnings**.

So, let's add these to our diagram. Please write "Sales/Revenue/Turnover" as a heading at the top of the rectangle, and then underneath this, write the heading of "Less Expenses." Then in the lower rectangle under our horizontal line, please write the heading "Bottom Line/Net Income/Profits/Earnings." This is illustrated on the next image:

```
┌─────────────────────────────────────────────┐
│    SALES / REVENUE / TURNOVER               │
│    LESS EXPENSES                            │
│                                             │
│                                             │
│                                             │
│                                             │
│                                             │
│                                             │
│─────────────────────────────────────────────│
│   BOTTOM LINE / NET INCOME / PROFITS / EARNINGS │
│                                             │
│                                             │
└─────────────────────────────────────────────┘
```

This report card is called an **Income Statement, a Profit & Loss Account, or a Statement of Operations**.

Do you remember how I said our first report card, our Balance Sheet, was like a photograph? Well, our second report card, our Income Statement is like a MOVIE, so you will see this report card title shown as Income Statement *for the period ended* ... 31 March, 30 June, 31 December, for example. This measures performance over a period of time. So let's now add a title at the top of our diagram, Profit and Loss account for the period ended ... See next image:

PROFIT AND LOSS ACOUNT
FOR THE PERIOD ENDED....

| SALES / REVENUE / TURNOVER |
| LESS EXPENSES |
| |
| NET INCOME |

Now, this report card is also known as a Theory, and as Keith says when he teaches this, "Here me now, believe me later!" You cannot spend your profits; you can only spend cash. Try going to a car dealership and showing them your income statement and say look, I made X number of pounds, euros, or dollars last year; I want that car. You are not going to drive that car away without paying hard cash for it!

Have you ever gotten to the end of a month and earned profits but did not have the cash to pay payroll, bills, taxes, etc.?

Well, profits and cash are two separate things.

> **Profit is a Theory;**
>
> **Cash is a Fact.**

Profits are an important theory, but it is just a theory – which leads us nicely onto our third and final report card, one which many business owners do not even see!

For your **Complimentary Financial Statement Demonstration** 5-Part video series to accompany the mastery steps in this book, while available, visit www.AlexParker.UK.com

PART 2

SECTION THREE

Understand Your Cash Flow Statements, Realize Your Cash Potential

> *The reason companies lose relevance,*
> *go broke,*
> *or fade into the sunset is because they*
> *continue to grow, but fail to evolve.*
> *– Keith Cunningham*

All too often, I have sat in a client meeting, saying, "You've had a great year; you've earned 'X' Well done." Then I run them through everything, leaving out no detail not worth bringing to light. Yet what occurs seemingly every time will be the same response. Aghast, my clients exclaim, "I've earned how much?! Where has it all gone!"

Well, this is where the title subject of this chapter comes in.

The Cash Flow Statement answers these very concerns, showing exactly what has happened with regard to the movement of cash. This is a principle that is so critical and yet often overlooked.

Most businesses do not fail for lack of income but instead for a lack of cash. Consider Enron for a moment; a classic example. The energy company was making great profits on paper, with all of the accounting adjustments taking place behind closed doors. But if you looked at their cash flow statements, you would find that they were *hemorrhaging* cash. They were funding their operations through financing rather than operations, a distinction which will become apparent in just a moment when I take you through our third and final report card of this section.

We just need to know where to look - which would be at the cash flow statement.

Most Accountants/CPAs do not even produce a cash flow statement; instead, they will likely only complete the two report cards already discussed: the Balance Sheet and Income Statement. Many business owners won't have even seen a Cash Flow Statement. Many accountants, myself included for many years, when completing the financial statements, will come to the section for the Cash Flow statement and will see the option "small and medium companies exempt from cash flow, tick here" in our accounts production software. And sure enough, we tick the option to claim exemption and just continue to only prepare the first two report cards, completely ignoring the final report card of the **Cash Flow Statement**.

So let's now look at this final report card.

Please draw a rectangle down the page, and this time split this into 3 equal parts by drawing two horizontal lines across our rectangle, the first a third of the way down and the second two-thirds of the way down. Please see the image below:

Now let's add some details. Not all cash is created equally. We have three main types of cash:

O Cash = cash generated or used by operations – for example, sales receipts or paying bills.

I Cash = cash generated or used by investing – for example, selling an asset or buying a new truck.

F Cash = cash generated or used by finance – for example, borrow money, or the investors add more cash, or we repay a loan or pay dividends.

So, let's add these details to our report card. In the top third of our rectangle, please write **Operations** – and I want you to exaggerate the "O" and make this much larger than the rest of the word. And to the right of this, please write a "+" sign and underneath the "+" sign, write a "–" sign. In the second section, please write **Investing**, and again please exaggerate the first letter "I" and make this much larger than the rest of the word Investing, just like we did for Operations. To the right of Investing, please write a plus and a minus, the plus being above the minus sign. Finally, in the third section, please write the word "**Finance**," and yes, you guessed it, please exaggerate the "F" of Finance to make this much larger, and again write a plus and minus to the right of the word Finance. So we now have our sections marked out, Operations, Investing, and Finance. Please see the next image:

OPERATIONS	±
INVESTING	±
FINANCE	±

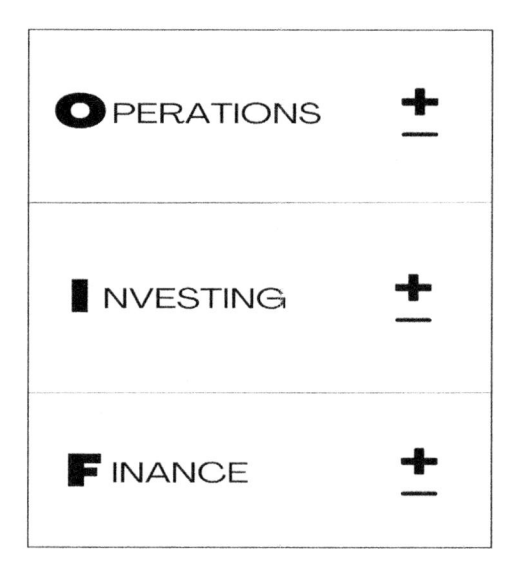

ONE of these types of cash is far more important than all the others – when I am teaching this in person, I draw a big red circle around the word Operations to highlight the fact that this is FAR more important than the other two types of cash. Please see the image below:

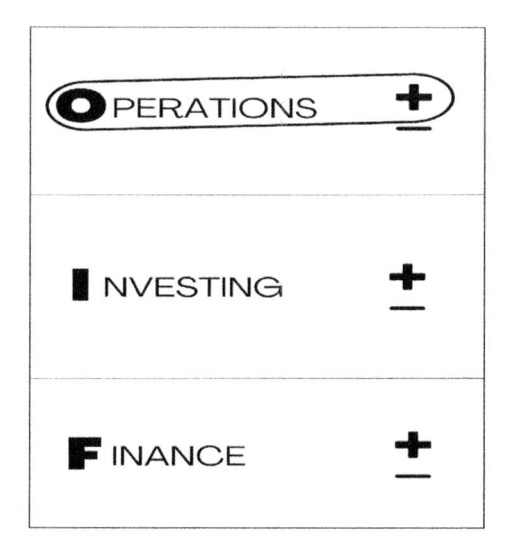

(**O**PERATIONS)	±
INVESTING	±
FINANCE	±

We can generate cash or we can spend cash, hence the plus and minus next to each heading in our Cash Flow Statement. For our cash from Operations, we will generate Operating cash flow when we receive payment from our customers after making a sale, and we will spend Operating cash when we pay a supplier. Similarly, we will spend Investing cash when we pay for a new piece of equipment, and we will generate Investing cash when we receive payment from a sale of a piece of equipment. And finally, we will generate Financing cash when we borrow new funds, and we will spend Financing cash when we make repayments of our loans, for example. In all these examples, please note this report card tracks the movement of cash, so for example we can make sales, but it is only when we receive payment of cash from our customers that this is then recorded in our Cash Flow Statement.

Sadly, most business owners do not even see this report card, much less manage their cash flow operations. Total cash flow is the sum of O cash, I cash, and F cash. Like the Income Statement, the Cash Flow Statement can be thought of as a MOVIE because, once again, this measures cash flow over a period of time, so you will see this report referred to as a Cash Flow Statement *for the period ended* ... 31 March, 30 June, 31 December, for example. So, let's now add a title to this report card, Cash Flow Statement for the Period Ended ... Please see next image:

CAHSFLOW STATEMENT FOR THE PERIOD ENDED....

Opening cash brought forward	X
OPERATIONS ±	X
INVESTING ±	X
FINANCE ±	X
Closing Cash	X

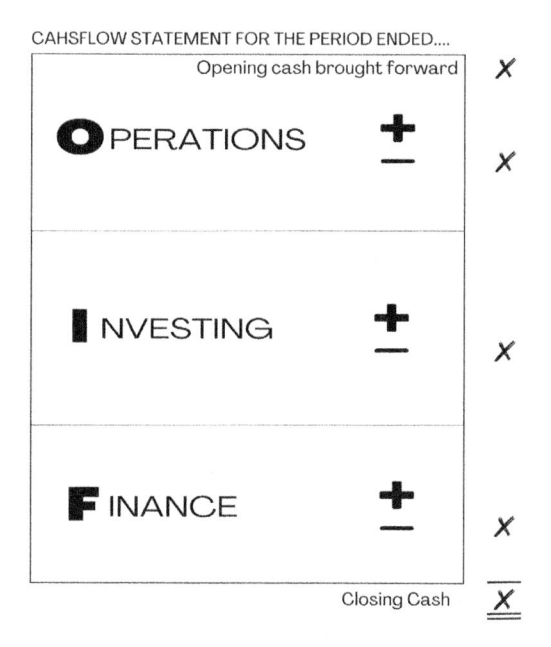

Let's tie all three report cards together. Just briefly, the whole point of having assets (Things and Stuff) in our businesses is to generate revenue to generate profits, which should then generate operating cash flow.

Assets are the resources of the business. These things and stuff can be physical resources such as property, plant and equipment, payroll dollars/euros or pounds or human resources such as labor resources, employees, contractors and/or your customer portfolio. We deploy these resources in a business to create revenue, which then creates profits and profits create cash flow. Cash is fundamental to business success.

It's cash flow that we need to focus on. But most people look at the profits instead. Profit is a theory, cash is a fact.

The degree to which a business is successful is the efficiency with which it deploys its resources to first create revenue. It's the efficiency of going from step to step that determines the ability of the business to thrive, not just survive. The business cycle is deploying assets to first create revenue, from which profits are generated which leads to the creation of cash flow.

Before we move on, let's look visually at how these three report cards fit together. Please see the image below:

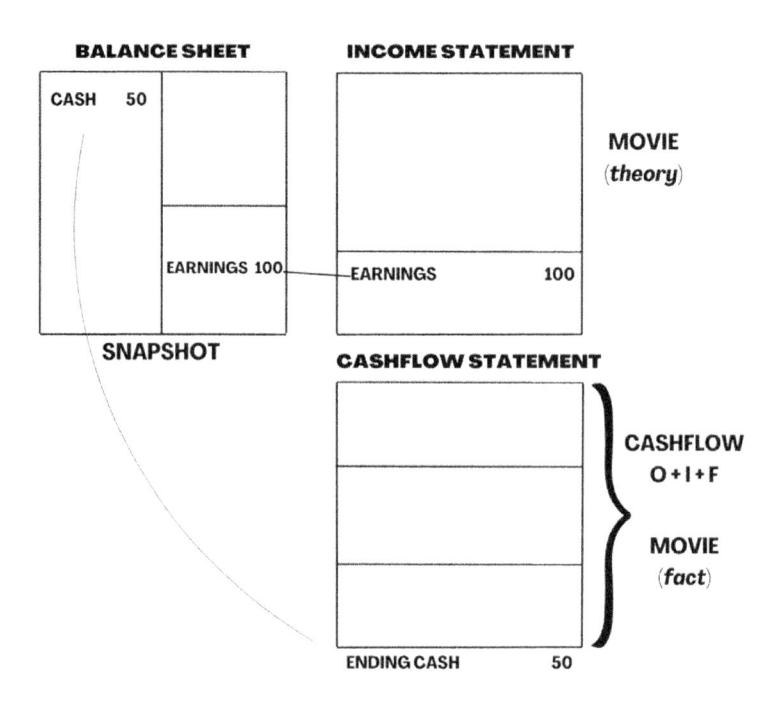

BALANCE SHEET

CASH   50

EARNINGS 100

SNAPSHOT

INCOME STATEMENT

EARNINGS   100

MOVIE (*theory*)

CASHFLOW STATEMENT

ENDING CASH   50

CASHFLOW O + I + F

MOVIE (*fact*)

You will see that the earnings at the bottom of the Income Statement flow through to the Earnings in the section in the

Balance Sheet for what we Own, and similarly, the final Cash balance from the cash Flow Statement flows through to the Cash recorded in Assets (Things and Stuff) on the Balance Sheet.

Do you remember me telling you about Enron earlier? This is one of the best examples I can think of in my career that illustrates the power of being able to read and understand the financial scorecards for a business.

If you looked at their Income Statement, this company was recording massive profits – but do you remember me sharing with you that the Income Statement is a Theory? Well, the accounting team was being, let's say, "creative" in their income recognition policies. If we look at the Cash Flow Statements of Enron prior to its collapse, we can see it was hemorrhaging Operating cash, and the bulk of its cash injections were coming from F cash, new finance, rather than cash generated from operations, which is not a sustainable model. Most businesses do not go bust due to a lack of profits but rather due to a lack of cash, and in particular, a lack of Operating cash. Operating cash is the actual creation process of the business, actual physical cash-generation. If a business owner goes into a car showroom and says, "I like that car. Here's my income statement. I'll give you a share of my future income", no salesman is going to say "Oh, yes. Here are the keys to the car." Instead they require a physical payment of cash to release the vehicle. This is the importance of understanding cash, the reality, vs. profits, the theory.

I hope you can see the ability to read and understand the financial statements for your business is a valuable skill to have in your toolkit. But I would like to share a few more final points regarding your financial statements before we move on to the final section of the book. As I mentioned, many businesses use their accounting report cards just to pay their taxes, but I'm here to tell you:

> **Your accounting report cards are to help you run your business, not just paying your taxes.**

Also, I should mention, there are two ways accountants and book-keepers prepare financial statements – on an **"accruals" basis** or a **"cash" basis**. Many businesses prepare their accounts on a cash basis for the purpose of paying their taxes, but this does not, in my opinion, give the valuable information that you need to run your business, so please *ensure you ask your accountants or book-keepers to prepare your business accounts on an accruals basis.*

Basically, on an accruals basis, income and expenses are recorded as they are earned and incurred – in other words, they are "matched" according to the time period being measured. On a cash basis, just like the name suggests, income and expenses are recorded only when cash changes hands, so if you receive payment from a large account, or many accounts at once you will get an impression of success, and when you pay a large bill, or several bills, you will appear to have big challenges.

It is critical that income and expenses are matched, which they are on an accrual basis, so that an accurate picture of your business performance can be seen.

How do we monitor and improve our business performance?
Two simple steps:

1. Measure our progress and results
2. Identify, correct and improve the activities causing those results

And then continually repeat the above 2 steps!

One last point to share. When you receive your business accounts from your accountants, chances are you will only receive one column of numbers, or if you're lucky two columns of numbers. This is of limited value, in my opinion.

The true value to be derived from financial data is by comparing **Trends** over time and in measuring the **relationship** between numbers within a given time period.

This is why any client I coach will receive reports with multiple time periods, so we can monitor the trends over time. They will also receive reports showing not just the numbers for each report card that I have described above, but the percentages showing the relationship of each expense number to sales revenue. For example, converting accounts receivable, inventory and accounts payable to a daily equivalent; all giving valuable information helping us to measure our progress and results and to identify, correct, and improve the activities causing those numbers.

This is too big a concept to fully cover here, but I did want to mention this and to highlight its importance, so that you can request this information from your accountants, or alternatively reach out to me for help as mentioned in the Next Steps section at the back of this book.

My aim in this section has not been to turn you into accountants; I just wanted to teach you the basic concepts for the 3 main dials in the cockpit of your business. I wanted you to have a rudimentary understanding of your business report cards so you can read and understand them better, to help you to organize your business data, to convert this into optics for your business so you can make better decisions, and ultimately, make more money.

So, how do we do this? I'll explain 3 basic yet powerful strategies to achieving this in the final section of my book.

I have prepared a set of videos to accompany this book demonstrating how to read financial statements and some basic levers you can pull in your business to maximise Operating cashflow. I feel this is such a critical area for every business to master and I feel video is a much more powerful way to present this information.

For your complimentary Financial Statement Demonstration videos, while available, please visit https://www.alexparker.uk.com/services/destiny-by-design-business-coaching

For your **Complimentary Financial Statement Demonstration** 5-Part video series to accompany the mastery steps in this book, while available, visit
www.AlexParker.UK.com

PART 3
BUSINESS STRATEGIES
TO
MOVE FORWARD

Here, you will use all the building blocks
provided to you up until this point
and learn how these can be brought together
within direct, immediately
applicable strategies
that will accelerate your business growth
in a sustainable way.

PART 3

SECTION ONE

Leverage in a Business

The Difference Between Income and Yield

> *Getting Everything You Can Out of All You've Got.*
> — Jay Abraham

So, just to recap for a moment: in the first section of my book, I highlighted the importance of cultivating and developing a strong mindset and psychology; and in the second section we covered reading and understanding the dials in the cockpit of our business (the financial statements). I believe these subjects set the foundation that allows me to share some of the levers we can pull in the cockpit of our business to make powerful improvements in its performance.

When I've attended some of my business events, we've been encouraged to repeat an incantation: "I love numbers and numbers love me." I could see many of my fellow business delegates had a lot of resistance to this at first, but this resonated so much with me because I do truly love numbers and the problems they allow us to solve.

By way of introduction to the section on business strategies, I want to share a story from my childhood. As a young child, I would ask my Dad for help with my math homework. My Dad is a mathematician; and he used to work for a large chemical company, and the chemists and physicists would come to him with a problem, with that he would create mathematical models to solve their challenges. I remember many nights sitting around our kitchen table feeling so frustrated, that he would always take me back to first principles. He would go through all the mathematical modeling principles, and he would show me at least 10 different ways of solving each question. I remember protesting and telling him I just wanted to know how best to answer each question.

What I did not realize at the time is that my Dad was not just helping me with my math homework; he was investing his time, energy, and expertise in preparing me for life – we have laughed together about this since.

I tell you this personal story from my childhood to illustrate my passion for paying this kindness from my Dad forward. I want to do the same for my audience. As an accountant, I don't want to just "crunch the numbers" for my clients and give them the "best" answer; I want to prepare them for the challenges of business so that they may thrive, not just survive.

If you are a person in business, or a fellow entrepreneur, then I believe we are brothers and sisters on the same path. The life of an entrepreneur can be a challenging life, but with the right tools in our toolkit, ultimately, it can be a rewarding journey. My personal belief is that we need to be Business Gladiators to survive the challenges in business, and my passion and purpose in writing this book is to stand on the shoulders of those who have gone before me, my mentors and indeed my clients who have entrusted me to guide them over the years, and to share the knowledge, experience, and expertise I have gathered with my audience.

I love the quote by Jay Abraham that I included at the start of this chapter: "Getting everything you can out of all you've got."

> **We all work hard in our businesses, but wouldn't it be better if we started to work *smarter* in our businesses?**

So, I want to introduce the concept that I describe as *leverage*.

What is leverage?

I always thought it was Aristotle that spoke of a lever and fulcrum, but when I was conducting my research for this book, I discovered that it was actually Archimedes that said: "Give me a place to stand, a fulcrum and a lever long enough and I shall move the world."

A fulcrum is an example of leverage. But leverage, per se, is anything that allows us to do more with less.

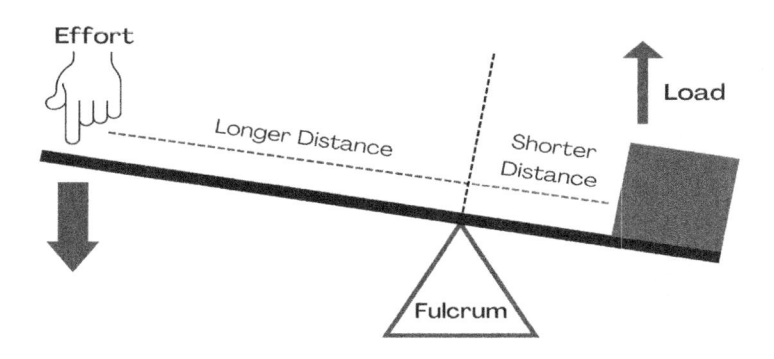

There is a limit to the weight that any of us can move, but if we employ a simple lever and fulcrum, we can move a far heavier weight with this strategy. Well, in a similar way, there are strategies that we can employ in our business to produce an out-sized gain for our efforts.

I believe there is power in simplicity – as Tony Robbins says, "Complexity is the enemy of execution." So with that in mind, please let me share with you the best definition of leverage that I have come across, which is from Keith Cunningham, who describes leverage as "simply any tool, technique or process that allows us to do more with less."

Before I describe my specific, simple business strategies to you, there are some basic concepts I want to share with you. Every business needs a healthy profit margin to survive. This may seem obvious, but I have seen many businesses with very low profit margins, and more often than not, these are not even monitored. Any client of mine will know I always focus on profit margins and ways to increase these all the time.

Second, and this leads me nicely to the first strategy I want to share with you, there is a distinct difference between "income" and "yield."

Everybody talks about income. **Income is absolute** – I made $10 today, I made $100 today, I made $1,000 today. It's an absolute number. Well, what they don't say is, *how did you produce that income?*

So a great example is a client of mine who works on long projects that take him about 4 years to complete and his profit margin is 20%. So his absolute profit on the project is 20%. But it takes him 4 years, so his yield is 5%. Because **yield is income per annum**. It's measured in time because time is valuable. Time is the one resource that all of us have the same amount of. And so it's really important to recognize the difference between income and yield rather than just looking at absolute terms.

If a business has two distinct product lines, and one product has a 10% profit margin and the other 20%, which one should we maximize? Well, before you answer, we need more information. If I tell you that the product line that has a 20% profit margin takes on average 4 years to deliver and the product with the 10% profit margin takes on average one year to deliver, now which one will you choose?

This demonstrates the importance of yield over income.

The product with the 20% profit margin in my example takes 4 years to deliver, so has a yield of 5% (20 divided by 4), whereas my 10% profit product has a yield of 10% (10 divided by one). Put simply; yield is income generated per annum – income is an absolute term, regardless of the time taken to earn it.

Taking this further, as I mentioned earlier, I always advocate to all my business clients the importance of maintaining healthy profit margins, but let's give another example. If a business model is such that the profit margins are only 5%, and the time taken to deliver the product or service is one month, the yield on the capital employed will be 60% (12 x 5% - 5% each month). So, for example, you could have a business with monthly sales of $1 million, making total sales for the year of $12 million, making profits of $600,000 with capital employed of $1 million.

In my mind, profit margins of only 5% is far too low and I use this example for illustration purposes only, but you can see that an income of 5% each month is an annual yield of 60%.

Now, if that same business has an alternative product offering with a 10% profit margin, but it takes 3 months to deliver, assuming everything else is equal. So now they make sales of $1 million each quarter with a profit margin of 10%. Well, the quarterly income will be $100,000 ($1 million @ 10%); over the year, this business will make total sales of $4 million with profits of $400,000.

So if we just compare the income or profit margins without considering yield, we may deploy our resources in the wrong direction.

I believe as business owners, our first objective is the quality of our services delivered to our customers; our clients come to us for the outcomes and results we provide to them.

> **But we also need to ensure we deploy our resources in the most efficient manner so we may continue to serve our clients well, provide for our families, and give to our communities.**

Business resources will be financial, labor, and or/equipment that we deploy in our business to generate an annual yield.

I hope I have shown that we need to understand the difference between income and yield when deciding how to deploy our business resources. This is a really important concept and one I always refer to when I teach my business coaching clients Optimisation and Maximisation strategies for their business.

But this is beyond the scope of this book because my mission in writing this book is to keep things simple. There is great power in simplicity, and my desire for you, dear reader, is for me to give you basic yet powerful strategies that you can implement in your business to produce outstanding improvements. However, if you decide to learn more about my more detailed strategies, I will include details at the end of this book of how you can learn more about how I guide my business clients to financial freedom and fulfillment.

And whilst speaking of Optimisation and Maximisation, there are many ways to grow a business, but many times business will only focus on pulling one lever if you like – growing sales!

However, I'm here to tell you, if you attempt to grow a business that is not optimized, very often you can grow your problems and inefficiencies leading to bigger problems, so the following simple strategies will help you start on this subject of Optimisation and Maximisation.

Leverage in a Business

Sales Strategy

The reason I took some time in Part 2 to go through how to read your financial statements is because now, when you draw out the following diagram, you should be able to immediately understand what I share with you.

Please draw out an Income Statement, which you will remember starts with a rectangle vertically down the page, with a horizontal line to separate the bottom third of the rectangle. Then please write "Sales" at the top of the rectangle, then write "Less Expenses" directly underneath sales and finally please write "Net Profits/Earnings" in the lower third, just as we did when I was sharing how to draw the Income Statement in the earlier section.

SALES / REVENUE / TURNOVER
LESS EXPENSES
BOTTOM LINE / NET INCOME / PROFITS / EARNINGS

Now for this example, we will start with Sales of 100, less expenses of 90, which will give us Net Profits of 10.

SALES	100
LESS EXPENSES	(90)
NET PROFIT / EARNINGS	10

This is a typical Income Statement showing gross Sales income of 100, Less Expenses of 90, giving a Net Income/Earnings of 10. This can be 100,000 or 100 million, and this can be pounds, euros, dollars, or any other currency; the concept is the same.

In my experience, most businesses have an average net profit of between zero and 20%, or to be more precise, most *profitable* businesses have a net profit of between zero and 20%, and so my example shows a net profit of 10%. But before you start to think, "Well my business has a bigger margin than that," the way I measure this is *after* the business owner has extracted his or her income, salary, dividends, etc. from the business.

So the first lever we can pull is to simply increase our prices by 5%, and there are a myriad of ways to achieve this; it is just a question of increasing the value proposition in the mind of our customer. If we increase our prices by 5%, our sales income now becomes 105. Our expenses remain 90 and so our earnings or bottom line now becomes 15 – a 50% increase by making just one small tweak in our business.

This, my friends, is the power of leverage in a business. See the next image:

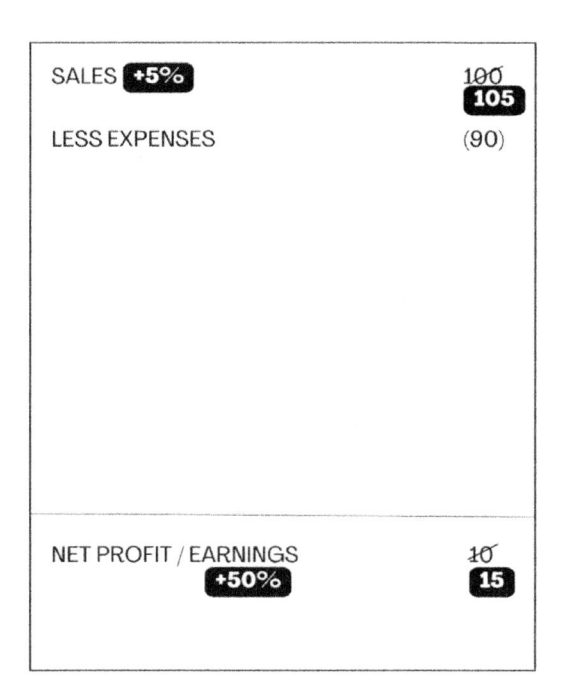

```
SALES  +5%                    ~~100~~
                              **105**
LESS EXPENSES                 (90)




NET PROFIT / EARNINGS         ~~10~~
       +50%                   **15**
```

Our sales income increases from 100 to 105 (thousand, million, £, €, $, etc.) and our bottom line, our net profits, increase from 10 to 15, a 50% increase. If this was your business making a bottom line of 100,000 per year, and we just increased your bottom line by 50,000, how would you feel now?

And there's more!

Please read on for Strategy #2 …

Leverage in a Business

Cost Strategy

> *Innovation basically involves making obsolete that which you did before.*
> – Jay Abraham

In our last strategy, we looked at an average business with total sales of 100, expenses of 90, with net profits or earnings of 10. Let's use this same example, but this time instead of looking to increase prices, let us look at how we can cut expenses.

> As business owners we ought to ask for each item of expense, "What is the ROI on this investment?"

Cutting expenses is often a matter of looking at overlooked simple things. For example, oftentimes clients have subscriptions that they've subscribed to that they no longer derive benefit from. I've seen so many businesses that have historic subscriptions to various publications which they no longer read for they are not creating an ROI (Return On Investment).

Another example of cutting expenses, if you visit Starbucks for instance to buy an expensive coffee every morning and afternoon, consider making your coffee in your office, or consider making a switch to a more healthy alternative - such as fresh water! This example may be more controversial to coffee lovers, but if you count up what you spend on your expensive Starbucks coffees over a year, it may shock you to discover how much this amounts to.

What we need to do is *change our mindset from expenses to investment.* If we think about the money we pay out as an investment on which we want a positive return, rather than overhead expenses, then we're in the right mindset. To undertake this strategy is so helpful.

If we cut our total expenses by just 10%, our expenses will reduce from 90 to 81, and our bottom line will increase from 10 to 19 – a 90% increase in our bottom line! Please see the next image:

SALES	100
LESS EXPENSES **-10%**	(~~90~~)
	81
NET PROFIT / EARNINGS **+90%**	~~10~~ **19**

Your net profit, or bottom line, is what's left after you incur all of the expenses for that period of time. If we managed to increase the net profit in your business from 100,000 to 190,000, how would you feel?

Accountants are often accused of knowing the cost of everything and the value of nothing. I believe that is because we will always start to help a business increase its performance by looking at cutting costs. The impact of this is one which can be felt immediately, whereas income generation strategies take longer to produce results.

I hope you see the power of the first two strategies I have shared, and of course, these strategies can be combined to achieve even greater improvements in business performance. We can increase prices AND reduce costs to pretty much double the bottom line for most businesses in fairly short order.

In my next strategy, I will share with you a simple and powerful strategy to propel and turbocharge your business growth to a completely new level. Ready? Then, please, read on ...

For your **Complimentary Financial Statement Demonstration** 5-Part video series to accompany the mastery steps in this book, while available, visit www.AlexParker.UK.com

PART 3

SECTION TWO

10-10-10 Strategy

> *As soon as you open your mind to doing things differently, the doors of opportunity practically fly off their hinges.*
>
> – Jay Abraham

I learned this strategy from Tony Robbins, and I believe he learned this from Jay Abraham. Tony asked Jay, "What are the 3 best simple steps any business can take to improve business performance?" And Jay listed the following 3 steps:

1. Increase the number of customers/clients

2. Increase the average transaction value (add more value)

3. Increase the frequency of repurchase (get more residual value from each customer)

In the case of my accounting business, where a lot of clients only buy once a year for their year-end work, you can replace step 3 of increasing the frequency of repurchase with increasing the number of referrals.

This strategy relies on the power of compounding. I believe Einstein is often quoted as saying the power of compounding was the eighth wonder of the world, but I believe the full quote is this:

> "Compound interest is the eighth wonder of the world. He who understands it, earns it ... he who doesn't ... pays it."

But what is compounding and why is it so powerful? The best example of this I recall was explained to me at a Tony Robbins' Business Mastery event. Please let me share this story with you now to illustrate the power of compounding.

Imagine you and I were playing a game of golf and I invited you to make a friendly bet of 10 cents on the first hole. Then let's say I suggested doubling the bet each hole. Would you take on this bet?

Imagine you did, and we go on to play 18 holes of golf. Do you know how much the bet will be on the 18th hole?

Well, let's do the math:

Hole 1 = 10 cents
Hole 2 = 20 cents
Hole 3 = 40 cents
Hole 4 = 80 cents

It's okay so far. Just a friendly bet, right?

Let's continue …

Hole 5 = $1.60
Hole 6 = $3.20
Hole 7 = $6.40
Hole 8 = $12.80
Hole 9 = $25.60

So we are halfway there and the bet is now $25.60 for the 9th hole. Before reading on, how much would you think the bet on the 18th hole will be? $100? $300? $500, maybe?

Well, let's carry on:

Hole 10 = $51.20
Hole 11 = $102.40
Hole 12 = $204.80
Hole 13 = $409.60
Hole 14 = $819.20

Now this is getting serious! But let's keep going:

Hole 15 = $1,638.40
Hole 16 = $3,276.80
Hole 17 = $6,553.60
Hole 18 = $13,107.20

Wow!

You can see by just starting with a modest bet of 10 cents on the first hole and just doubling the bet each hole, we have a massive bet of over $13,000 for the final hole. This, my friends, is the power of compounding!

I feel pictures speak a thousand words, so here is a graph to demonstrate this pictorially:

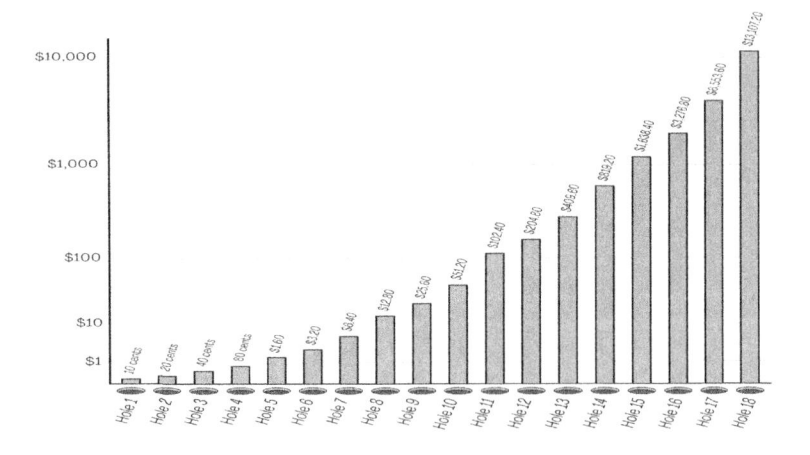

You will note that in the beginning, the growth is modest. Even at the halfway point, the bet is only $25.60. However, there comes a point when the growth accelerates, and then the growth becomes exponential.

I hope this concept excites you as to how you can employ this in your business. So, how can we employ the power of compounding in our business? Please let me share with you Jay Abraham's Three Ways to Grow a Business Model.

First, please let me stress we are just going to focus on the "What" for now; the "How" always comes after "What" and "Why" in any business strategic planning.

So, let's take a simple small company example:

Current Number of Customers		Current Average Transaction Value		Current Repurchase Frequency or Referrals		Total
1,000	x	$100	x	2	=	$200,000

Now, let's apply a 10% increase to each of the 3 categories. This is usually my starting point with my clients, which is why I refer to this as the 10-10-10 strategy. If we increase 3 categories by 10% each, we will get a 30% total increase, right? Wrong! Let's see:

10% Increase		*10% Increase*		*10% Increase*		*33.1% Increase*
1,100	x	$110	x	2.2	=	$266,200

Because of the power of compounding, just by making 10% tweaks in 3 categories for our business, we get an overall increase of 33.1%!

So, what would happen if we made a larger increase? Let's see:

20% Increase		20% Increase		20% Increase		72.8% Increase
1,200	x	$120	x	2.4	=	$345,600

So if we made a 20% increase in all 3 categories, we do not get a 60% overall increase; our total increase will be 72.8%. Are you starting to see the power of compounding at work? Are you starting to get excited about what this could mean for your business?

Let me give you one final example:

33% Increase		25% Increase		50% Increase		150% Increase
1,330	x	$125	x	3	=	$498,750

I hope you can see that this simple strategy can produce exponential results. And this isn't even the best part! The best part is that this is not a "one and done" strategy; this can be repeated over and over to generate powerful growth and scaling.

When I first introduce this concept to clients, I am often asked: "Well, what about for larger companies, will this work for larger businesses?" Of course it will, it is simply a matter of mathematics. Let me show you:

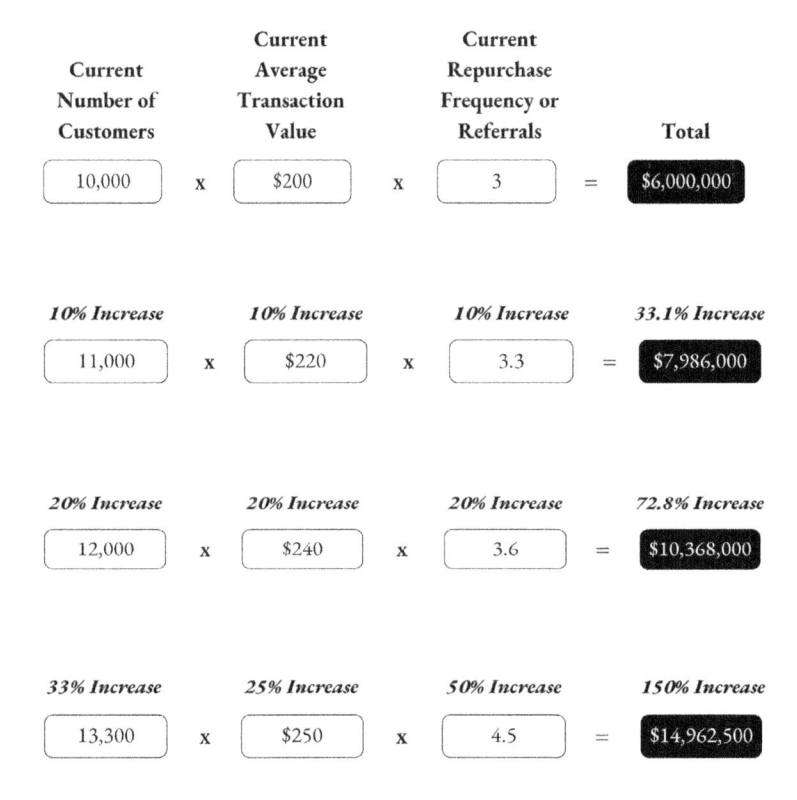

Current Number of Customers		Current Average Transaction Value		Current Repurchase Frequency or Referrals		Total
10,000	x	$200	x	3	=	$6,000,000

10% Increase		10% Increase		10% Increase		33.1% Increase
11,000	x	$220	x	3.3	=	$7,986,000

20% Increase		20% Increase		20% Increase		72.8% Increase
12,000	x	$240	x	3.6	=	$10,368,000

33% Increase		25% Increase		50% Increase		150% Increase
13,300	x	$250	x	4.5	=	$14,962,500

If this was YOUR business, how would you feel with this level of increased growth this year?

And next year?

And the year after?

Are you starting to see the power of this simple strategy? So, now let's apply this to a real-world example – *your* business!

For the purpose of this exercise, if you don't know your exact numbers, just use your closest estimate for now. I just want you to enter your own numbers so you start to get an insight into what this could mean for your business.

So, for example, if you know your sales revenue is approximately $100,000 and you know you have approximately 500 customers, and your average transaction value is $100, then on average, each customer must buy twice in a year – 500 x 100 x 2 = $100,000.

Phase 1: Now, fill out the numbers for your own business below:

Current Number of Customers		Current Average Transaction Value		Current Repurchase Frequency or Referrals		Total Sales Revenue
☐	x	☐	x	☐	=	☐

Phase 2: 10-10-10 Plan: Calculate a 10% increase for each box for a total increase in sales income of 33.1%

10% Increase in number of customers		10% Increase in average transaction value		10% Increase in frequency of repurchase/referrals		33.1% Increase
☐	x	☐	x	☐	=	☐

Phase 3: Now create a more aggressive target plan:

This is your plan, so you get to choose this bit. You can choose my previous examples of a 33-25-50 plan to create a 150% total sales increase or if you want to be more conservative, try a 20-20-20 plan for a 72.8% increase or choose any figure of your choice. Let's go!

Increase in number of customers		Increase in average transaction value		Increase in frequency of repurchase/referrals		Total
☐	x	☐	x	☐	=	☐

So, what did you choose? Did you decide on a 20-20-20 plan, a 33-25-50 plan, or one of your own making? Now let me ask you: how would you FEEL achieving these results in your business THIS year?

Please remember, this is an exercise that can be repeated over and over to generate the exponential growth we aspire to.

And one final point on this strategy, if you have different revenue streams within your business, you can create a different growth plan for each revenue stream.

As I mentioned earlier, I feel strongly that when approaching any new concept, it is important to focus on "What" we want to achieve and "Why" it is a must for us. This is the power, the fuel that will keep us driving forward when we encounter obstacles and challenges.

So, this is my challenge to you before we move forward to the final chapter. Please, take a moment to write down WHAT it is you want for your business for the next 12 months and

WHY it is so important to create this for yourself, your business, your family, and your life.

The "How" of this particular exercise goes beyond the "simple" structure that I have endeavored to create for this book, but I never want to leave anyone hanging for more support. So if you would like to work more closely on implementing such a plan for your business, I will include details of how you could explore the opportunity to work with me as part of my business group to help you implement the strategies outlined in this book in your business and your life.

This leads me to the final simple strategy that I want to share with you to help you create your sustainable success …

PART 3

SECTION THREE

Build A Cash Machine

I believe all of us in business need to have a second business, separate and distinct from our main business. A business without any employees, which is highly automated to generate cash.

So many of us these days are consumers. As an example, we buy Apple iPhones, iPads, etc. But how many of us own stock in Apple, the company that makes the products we buy?

In this final strategy, which again builds upon the power of compounding. I will encourage you to consider becoming owners and *investors*, instead of only consumers.

The simple essence of this strategy is to take a percentage of what we earn, set this aside each month for our future self, and let the fund grow compounded to create a position where we do not have to work; we work because we want to!

Anyone can do this, whether they have a business or not. We just need to decide what percentage of our earnings we will save and invest, and then the key is to AUTOMATE it!

Do you remember my example of the game betting on each golf hole? And do you remember that in the beginning, the growth was very modest, and then, you reach a point where the growth accelerates? Well, this strategy is very similar. It may take some time to build momentum, but there will come a time when you will hit a critical mass to produce an income for life.

I heard the amazing story of Theodore Johnson at a Tony Robbins' Business Mastery event. Theodore was a UPS worker earning a salary of no more than $14,000 each year and yet, in his old age, was worth more than $70 million! But how did he achieve this?

A good friend of his convinced him to set aside 25% of his salary consistently every month to build a cash machine. At first, he pushed back and resisted such a suggestion, but his friend convinced him by saying if the government increased taxes by 25%, he would be really upset and complain about it, but would ultimately pay it. With this, his friend convinced him to commit to this discipline of saving 25% of his salary every month. Now, he chose to invest most of this into UPS stock, the company at which he worked, and due to the power of compounding, this grew to an amazing total.

I believe Theodore retired in 1952, so a $14,000 annual salary back then was worth a lot more than $14,000 today, but nonetheless, this is a powerful example of what is possible if we commit to a disciplined strategy of saving the first 20-25% of our income to build a fund to provide passive income. Once this passive income provides for our daily living expenses, we can achieve financial freedom.

Also, I believe Theodore chose to invest all of his savings into one stock, UPS. Now, whilst I can't give financial advice, I would never want to put all my eggs in one basket; I would prefer to choose a well-diversified stock portfolio. I only cite this story of how someone with a fairly modest means created a vast amount of wealth by adopting a simple strategy that works – and one which we can emulate to achieve our goals for financial freedom.

At Tony Robbins' Wealth Mastery event, we are taught we only need 4 things to achieve wealth:

- Time
- Compound growth
- Intelligent decisions
- Some money

In its simplest terms, we need to spend less than we earn and invest the difference.

You and I are already money machines. We work hard and we get paid for our efforts. We then get to choose what we do with the money we earn. Will we spend it all so that it's gone from our grasp, or will we decide to take some portion of our earnings and invest this for our future self? It's this simple. And I would suggest this is the most important financial decision all of us can make – so choose wisely!

Also, one point to stress with this strategy: the earlier you start, the bigger your nest egg will become. To illustrate this point, let's consider two different investors:

> **John** starts at age 19 and saves $300 per month and then stops investing when he's 27 years old and leaves his fund to compound in a tax-free environment at 10% per year. His total investment is $28,800 (8 years @ $3,600 per annum).
>
> **Steve** starts saving at the age of 27, and he also invests $300 per month. He also invests in a tax-free environment, compounding at 10% per year, but he continues to invest until he's 65, so his total investment is $140,400 (39 years at $3,600 per annum).

Which investor do you think grows the biggest retirement pot? Well, at first glance, you might expect the investor who has invested $140,000 rather than just $29,000, but in actual fact, due to the power of compounding, John, who only invested $29,000 over 8 years creates a fund of $1,867,287 at 65, whereas Steve who invested $140,000 over 39 years grows a fund of $1,589,733 at 65.

So, the moral of the story is: *the earlier we start, the bigger the nest egg we will be able to grow.*

The above example was presented to me at one of the many Tony Robbins' Business Mastery events I have been blessed to attend, and I always want to give credit to the source of my learning.

So, my questions to you are:

- When will you start? – I suggest NOW!
- And how much will you save? – I'd like to encourage you to save 20-25% of your earnings, but if this seems high to start with, start with 5% or 10% and then you can increase this over time, especially once you start implementing the business strategies that I shared with you earlier which can help you to achieve exponential growth in your business.

> *The most important decision*
> *I believe you can make*
> *is to start **NOW**!*

It is also important to consider asset allocation and diversification, but I believe this is a complex area and I am focused so powerfully on *simple* strategies in this book, so I feel this is a subject beyond its scope of this book. However, I do want to just touch upon the subject of my "3 bucket" approach to investing.

I believe we should all consider having 3 separate buckets for our savings:

SECURITY/PEACE OF MIND BUCKET
Low Risk / Low Return Investment

GROWTH/RISK BUCKET
High Risk / Higher Return Investment

DREAM BUCKET
Money to spend on our dream

And we all need to decide the allocation of our savings between each bucket. Those of us who are a little older will usually choose a higher percentage of savings in Bucket Number 1, our Security/Peace of Mind bucket; and those who are a little younger, with many more working years ahead, may choose to allocate a higher percentage to the Growth/Risk Bucket since if this doesn't work out, you still have plenty of time to recover. But I believe all of us need some allocation to our Dream Bucket in order to enjoy experiences that make our hearts sing!

So, it's decision time again. What percentages of your savings will you allocate to each bucket? It doesn't matter what you decide; you can change this as you go along. The most important decision you can make is to START NOW!

CONCLUSION

My intention in writing this book has been to share simple, proven, and powerful techniques that, upon reading my book, all readers will be able to say to themselves, "This makes sense; let me put this into practice in my business NOW!"

So to recap, I mentioned that in my experience, it doesn't matter how powerful the business strategies I share are; without the right mindset, they will not get implemented – and my focus has been on helping you to achieve real, tangible results!

This is why the first section of my book has focused on mindset and psychology. To give you a strong foundation, to give you the best opportunity to successfully implement what I shared later in the book.

Second, you may remember the great analogy I shared for those of us who walk the path of a business entrepreneur is to compare it to a pilot flying a plane. Just like the pilot has a vast array of dials in his cockpit, giving him valuable information and he has levers he can pull to change his direction and ultimately arrive at his chosen destination, we also have dials in the cockpit of our business, namely our financial scorecards. We need to understand what they are telling us, which is why I shared with you the teachings I learned from the wonderful Keith Cunningham to help you to read and understand your financial scorecards. I've also recorded a video presentation of this important topic to help you understand these teachings.

A plane is off course for most of its journey, and it's only with the pilot's input with correctional action throughout the journey that allows it to arrive at its destination. And so in the third part of my book, I have shared some simple, but powerful, strategies to allow you, as the pilot of your business, to change course towards achieving your financial freedom.

The emphasis of my book has been to provide simple strategies; those 2-millimeter shifts that, when extrapolated over time, make profound impacts on our trajectory.

My passion has been to provide proven and achievable strategies for all readers to achieve outstanding results, and for those who want more, I stand ready to assist with a vast array of additional resources – from digital products, business forums, and even one on one coaching for the super-ambitious!

It has been an honor and a privilege to share with you the first steps to what I have learned and crafted over my career. If we never meet again, I hope I have added value to you, which you can now implement to create your own Sustainable $uccess. May God bless you all and I hope and pray I get the opportunity to assist you in new and exciting ways. Yes, now you're ready!

NEXT STEPS

> *A good business strategist has the ability to save livelihoods, save marriages, and save lives.*
>
> *– Alex Parker*

If you're busy as a business owner, I want you to ask yourself a few questions:

- Are you ready to stop just spinning your wheels and instead become productive in your business?
- Do you have the desire to work efficiently and work smarter rather than harder?
- Are you ready to be happier by improving the results and not just achieving the same results each year?
- Do you want your whole team to be more efficient and productive?

If any of your answers to the above questions are yes, then we need to measure in order to manage. Remember, what doesn't get measured won't be managed.

Having your annual financial statements prepared for governmental filings and tax calculation is the first step, not the *end* step. Most accountants are taught that that's the finished product, but as an entrepreneur, I believe that's only the first step.

Most entrepreneurs receive their year-end accounts at least six months after the year; they are six to eighteen months out of date by then. A business needs management information, and in my opinion, they need this monthly, so they've got time to make changes.

If you have a problem in your business, and you're only measuring results each year, you will have a bad year.

If you're measuring quarterly, you will have a bad quarter.

And if you're measuring monthly, you may have a bad month.

You can even measure weekly to discover problems and challenges earlier and take corrective action.

But it's not just the financial statements; it's looking at what we call **Key Performance Indicators (KPIs)** and the performance of individual sections of the business.

Rather than just having documents for tax filing, you can have business strategic advice to pilot your business to your chosen destination. This is how you create the business you need to have the life you really want.

If you would like more information on having a business strategy session about going one step further, contact us at www.AlexParker.UK.com.

On a broader coaching assignment, first of all, we need to optimize *and* maximize the results. If you grow a business that is not performing well, you create more problems and you exaggerate what is currently happening in the business, both good and bad. Whereas if you first take the time to optimize and maximize the efficiency of the business, when you then grow and scale, you grow and scale with those efficiencies.

But the only way to know if a business is efficient and productive is to measure more than just the figures in our year-end financials.

You could increase the bottom line if you have increased efficiencies, which means that you don't necessarily have to be present in the business as much.

For instance, before my business was efficient, I was working seven days a week, 24/7. Now I'm introducing efficiencies, whereby I've increased the resources in my business, and they are controlled with certain metrics. So there are targets for those resources to achieve, which means that I don't have to be in the business 24/7. I can actually create a balance and have a life outside of the business. If the business is more efficient, then I can use the resources the business generates for good deeds in the time that I'm not in the business – and that is very important to me.

People have different drivers, but I think we all want to do well in life. In my experience, many people in business are good at the business that they operate, but they are perhaps *not as good* at the business end of doing what they do. And that's where I believe I have the expertise and experience to bring to help you improve in those areas in the business end of what you do.

> *By working with me,*
> *you can increase that muscle,*
> *build those skills,*
> *make more money in your business,*
> *and have more time for your life.*

I know, personally, the pain of an experience where business doesn't work well. I've come through that, and so that's very much a driving force behind me.

A friend of mine told me the story that he no longer has his father because, when his father got into trouble in his business, his accountant didn't step up when he needed him to. A family is deprived of a husband and a father, all because he didn't have the professional support that he needed when he was going through a really tough time with his business. So if I can just save one person, then it's all been worthwhile.

Obviously, making more money is one of the outcomes, but I believe, with the service I bring to bear, it's not just about increasing income. It's very much about increasing fulfillment, which is why I put this in my business strapline – *I help guide my clients to their financial freedom and fulfillment.*

Without overstating it, I believe a good business strategist has the ability to save livelihoods, save marriages, and save lives. I know through the COVID-19 period, I stepped up strongly and helped people pivot into new directions when their livelihoods were under threat. Think of the story I just shared with you about my friend and his father. Some people can't cope with their livelihood being threatened, and then they are no longer here for their family. It is extremely powerful the ripple effect or potential ripple effect of what I bring to the table.

> *That's why I'm so passionate about it –*
> *It's not just creating extra pounds,*
> *dollars, or euros;*
> *It's about creating beautiful lives.*

Step 1: For your **Complimentary Financial Statement Demonstration** video to accompany the impact mastery steps in this book, while available, visit
https://www.alexparker.uk.com/services/destiny-by-design-business-coaching

Step 2: Join Now! The Destiny by Design Facebook group https://www.facebook.com/profile.php?id=100057101363738. Members receive special trainings directly from Alex and his team. Members receive even more nuances of the 2% Shifts for *Sustainable* $uccess.

Step 3: Sign up for our free Financial Empowerment Letter for your Destiny By Design journey at www.AlexParker.UK.com. You will also be notified about the live and virtual Destiny by Design Business Summits.

The fact that you read, and hopefully applied the lessons in this book tells me that you are really serious about taking your business to the next level. You get to:

Step 4: Become a part of The Financial Platinum Mastermind, a community of like-minded business owners that are ready to be guided to the next level of financial freedom and fulfillment.

Step 5: If you are ready to take the master leap forward, 1:1 coaching may be for you. Contact Alex at https://www.alexparker.uk.com/contact-us to have the conversation.

ABOUT THE AUTHOR

Alex Parker, Chartered Accountant and your *Destiny by Design*™ Business Strategist lives in a lovely village called Lymm, Cheshire, United Kingdom. His beautiful labrador, Ruby, fills his heart with her gentle, loving spirit every day.

Alex loves to help and serve people at the highest level. He consistently attends high-level training to bring the best, most up-to-date strategies to his clients, such as being a Platinum Partner with Tony Robbins.

When not serving his clients, he's serving on the tennis court. He enjoys cooking healthy foods and working out to increase energy for a more fulfilled life.

Printed in Great Britain
by Amazon